MANHATTAN PUBLIC LIBRARY DISTRICT

3 8001 00076 4245

W9-CEK-170

OCT 4 2007

Second Edition

10 09 08 07 06   5 4 3 2 1

Copyright © 2006 JRL Publications, LLC

All rights reserved. No part of this book may be reproduced or transmitted in any
manner whatsoever without the written permission of the publisher, except as personal
copies not for resale or distribution, for use only by owners of a copy of this book.

Published by
Gibbs Smith, Publisher
P.O. Box 667
Layton, Utah 84041

Orders: 1.800.748.5439
www.gibbs-smith.com

Created by: **Jeanette R. Lynton**

Executive Director: **Kristine Widtfeldt**

Creative Manager: **Kristy McDonnell**

Art Director: **Eric Clegg**

Graphic Designer: **Alison Meyers**

Writers: **Stephanie Olsen, JoAnn Jolley, Tori Bahoravitch**

Editor: **Brandi Rainey**

Photographer: **Derek Israelsen**

Photo Stylist: **Diane Call**

Printed and bound in Hong Kong

Thank you to all the talented stamp artists who helped make my beautifully simple
layout concepts come to life.

For information about the products used in these layouts, please contact a Close To My
Heart Consultant by calling 888.655.6552, or visiting www.closetomyheart.com.

First Edition Published by JRL Publications, LLC. ISBN: 0-9771668-0-5

Library of Congress Control Number: 2006924883

ISBN 1-4236-0154-8

Lori Brown, Ind. Consultant
ph. 815-478-5119
www.loribrown.myctmh.com

Cherish

SCRAPBOOK LAYOUTS MADE BEAUTIFULLY SIMPLE

Gibbs Smith, Publisher
Salt Lake City

MANHATTAN PUBLIC LIBRARY DISTRICT

Dear Friends:

Since I first began scrapbooking as a young girl, I have delighted in celebrating the precious moments of my everyday life. For me, remembering the people and experiences I cherish is one of life's greatest joys, and through time, I've learned that helping others scrapbook their cherished memories is just as fun! My lifelong passion for scrapbooking and sharing my techniques culminated in the founding of Close To My Heart, a company that I'm proud to say is a true leader in the scrapbooking industry.

In the mid nineties, I completed the first volume in Close To My Heart's scrapbooking "how to" series, the *Reflections Scrapbook Program*™, which was devoted to teaching my basic scrapbooking concepts. I wanted to ensure that the program included simple diagrams and easy-to-follow instructions, to make completing elegant scrapbook pages fast and easy for people of all ages, interests, and creative abilities. The original concepts I included in *Reflections* have become the basis of scrapbooking with Close To My Heart. Through the years additional volumes have followed, each building on *Reflections'* foundation.

Now, with great excitement and enthusiasm, I give you my newest scrapbooking "how to," *Cherish*. This wonderful guide reflects the evolution of my original page concepts, and illustrates what I love most about scrapbooking: the opportunity it gives us to honor, remember, and strengthen the relationships we share. As you delve into these beautifully designed pages, my hope is that you will find joy in the simple act of creating.

Cherish contains 50 fabulous two-page concepts, each one beautiful, unique, and simple to re-create. Follow the cutting diagrams and step-by-step instructions to put together eye-catching layouts in just minutes, or mix and match concepts for an infinite number of possibilities. So doing, you will quickly build a lasting tribute to the people and experiences you cherish most.

Sincerely,

Jeanette

JEANETTE R. LYNTON

Since the 1970s, Jeanette has enjoyed a passion for preserving treasured memories, and early in life began creating exclusive stamps and sharing her scrapbooking ideas. Today, Close To My Heart, the company Jeanette founded, is a leader in the scrapbooking and stamping industry.

Always at the forefront of innovation and creativity, Jeanette's new products have included the world's first true 12" x 12" scrapbooking format; a series of instructional programs offering simple guidelines for dynamic scrapbook layouts and homemade cards; scrapbooking kits featuring pre-printed layouts, and My Acrylix,™ clear decorative stamps and blocks that allow for perfect stamp placement.

Jeanette's artistic eye and "let me show you how" philosophy have made scrapbooking faster, simpler, and easier than ever before, while continuing to enhance the art of preserving memories and celebrating relationships.

3 8001 00076 4245

So Sweet

"I love cookies!"

Tea Party

The Joys of Scrapbooking

Memories are the essence of our life's experiences, and preserving them is one of the great keys to making life richer and more meaningful. What do you remember about your last vacation? Your wedding day? The home you grew up in? It's amazing how quickly the small details can be forgotten if they're not recorded. A personalized scrapbook album is absolutely the best place to preserve the photographs, record the details, and save the memorabilia that tell your life's story. Your scrapbook is a legacy that can be shared with family, friends, and generations yet to come.

HOW TO USE THIS BOOK

Cherish is dedicated to helping you preserve your memories in unique and creative ways. Using a host of simple design concepts and easy-to-follow instructions, you'll be able to fashion beautiful layouts in record time. Each design is flexible enough to allow for a variety of photo sizes and placements, assembly preferences, color combinations, and embellishments.

Although each concept is presented as a two-page layout, you can rotate the pages—one or both pages a single or multiple turns, swap them left to right, or even mix a page from one concept with a second page from another, to create unique layout combinations all your own. (See page eight for color illustrations of ways you can mix and match my page concepts to fit your photos or creative inclinations.) Soon you'll become an expert at putting your own touches to your pages.

In addition, separate sections at the back of the book describe (1) special tips and techniques that will add fun and excitement to your pages, and (2) recipes for each layout that will help you choose dynamic color combinations, Background & Texture (B&T) papers, and accessories to make your pages really stand out in a crowd!

GETTING STARTED

There are many ways to organize an album, and you may find yourself combining different methods or creating each album in a different way. Consider the following options:

Chronological: Scrapbook the events of your life in order of occurrence. This is truly a record of your life—day by day, month by month, or year by year.

Topical: Organize your album by topic, with one section for each event or style of page.

Topics may include Christmas, vacations, family members, pets, or school days—whatever is important and relevant to you.

Thematic: As you organize your thoughts and photos, is there one event or theme that stands out? Capture it in an album all its own! Theme albums clearly emphasize what means the most to you.

THE IMPORTANCE OF QUALITY PRODUCTS

As you select and purchase products to use in your albums, it's important to use only those that help to preserve your memories for long-term enjoyment. Be sensitive to the following items as you create, but don't let them distract you from the true joys of scrapbooking—preserving memories and finding an outlet for your creative flair.

Archival: Archival products are free of those elements that over time will deteriorate your precious memories. Use only archival safe materials in your scrapbook.

Acid-free: Acid is a harmful, destructive element that will ruin a scrapbook page and photos over time. Try to avoid including any acidic elements in your scrapbook.

Lignin-free: Always select lignin-free paper for your scrapbook—paper which has had all lignin (the natural acidic glues found in wood pulp) removed. Most lignin-free paper is also buffered, meaning it contains an additional layer of protection for your photos and memorabilia.

Harmful Environments: Whenever possible, keep your scrapbook away from direct heat, prolonged exposure to direct light and sunlight, and moisture or humidity. Store your albums in a location that is accessible yet protected. Your albums will last longer if they are stored closed and in an upright position.

CHOOSING YOUR PAPERS

Selecting your B&T paper and cardstock is a matter of personal preference—you may like stark color contrast and vibrant patterns to express your personality, or you may prefer working with monochromatic shades that give distinction and elegance to your photos. Or perhaps you like to mix it up a little!

To guide you, this book includes recommendations for paper selections—which pieces should be cut from solid-color cardstock, and which components work best in B&T papers. If you're just getting started, I suggest you follow the paper recommendations for best results. As you become more confident adapting the concepts to your style and photos, you may also want to experiment with your paper selections.

PHOTO MATTING

Matting adds dimension and beautiful layering to your scrapbook pages—but not all photos need to be matted, particularly when you're working with many photos on a single page or when your photos are very small. *Cherish* includes concepts that feature layouts with and without photo matting for variety and emphasis. As you work with the concepts, you may elect to crop a photo a bit smaller than the recommended photo size in order to set it off with a mat. Feel free to use the photo boxes in the way that best showcases your memories.

JOURNALING & TITLE BOXES

Memories fade, and sometimes even your favorite photos can't help you fully recall a story. That's why every scrapbook layout needs a title and a journal entry to capture the story behind the photos and to give the page a focal point and visual balance. Each concept in *Cherish* indicates a recommended title and journaling space—sometimes you'll wish to combine the two together, other times you may wish to separate them so that the title anchors the page and the journaling box is near the photos it describes. As you prepare your photos for placement in the concept, decide how you want to use the title and/or journaling boxes indicated, then crop and place your photos accordingly.

EMBELLISHMENTS

Embellishments, from adding simple brads to high-end art techniques, can make your layouts come alive. Each concept in this book features simple schematics—without embellishments—to make the concept easy to follow and duplicate. However, you'll also see that each concept includes a finished sample layout that showcases an innovative technique and embellishment tips. I encourage you to try your hand at these techniques and to have fun selecting a mix of embellishments that will transform your layouts into works of art!

One Concept—Infinite Possibilities

Each two-page layout in this book has been designed for maximum creativity. Every page can be rotated or swapped, giving you an infinite number of layout combinations. The three two-page layouts on this page were all created using the same *Cherish* concept, yet all three have very distinctive appearances.

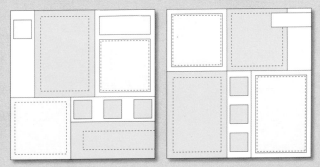

Dramatic Fashion Concept

These layouts were designed according to the original concept instructions and diagrams. For variety, these pages feature a different theme and color palette than illustrated on page 82.

In this concept variation, each page was rotated 180 degrees. Notice how rotating the left-hand page gives the layout title prominence because it appears at the top of the page instead of the bottom. Rotating the right-hand page allowed the portrait of the soldier to appear in the upper-left corner, immediately drawing the eye.

In the final example, each page was rotated one-quarter turn counter-clockwise and then placed in reverse order so the left page concept now appears on the right. The original concept was designed for several vertical photos but by rotating the pages, horizontal photos can easily be used instead.

Quick Reference

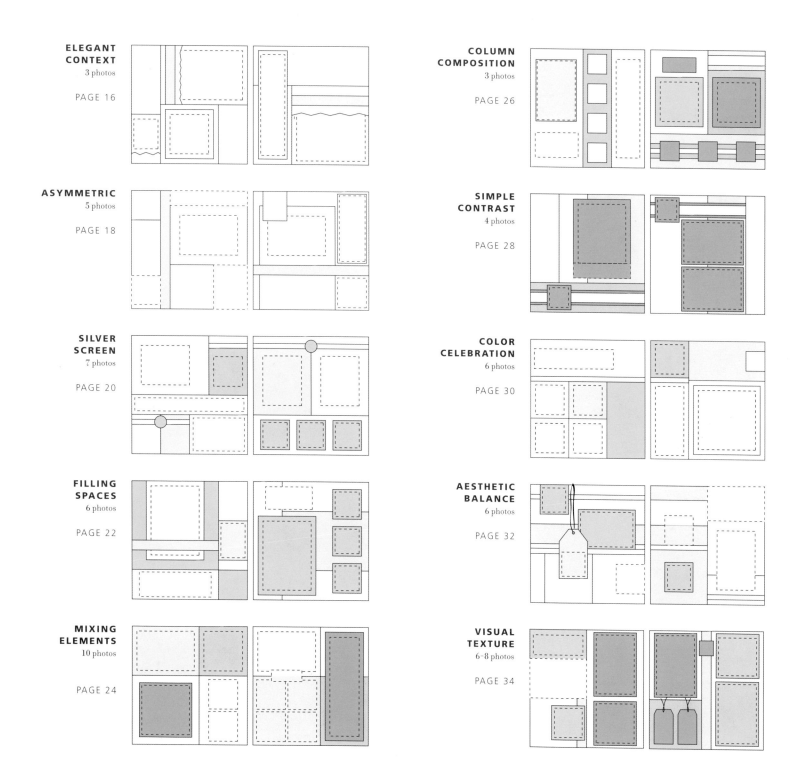

ELEGANT CONTEXT
3 photos

PAGE 16

ASYMMETRIC
5 photos

PAGE 18

SILVER SCREEN
7 photos

PAGE 20

FILLING SPACES
6 photos

PAGE 22

MIXING ELEMENTS
10 photos

PAGE 24

COLUMN COMPOSITION
3 photos

PAGE 26

SIMPLE CONTRAST
4 photos

PAGE 28

COLOR CELEBRATION
6 photos

PAGE 30

AESTHETIC BALANCE
6 photos

PAGE 32

VISUAL TEXTURE
6-8 photos

PAGE 34

9

© 2005 JRL PUBLICATIONS

© 2005 JRL PUBLICATIONS

Quick Reference

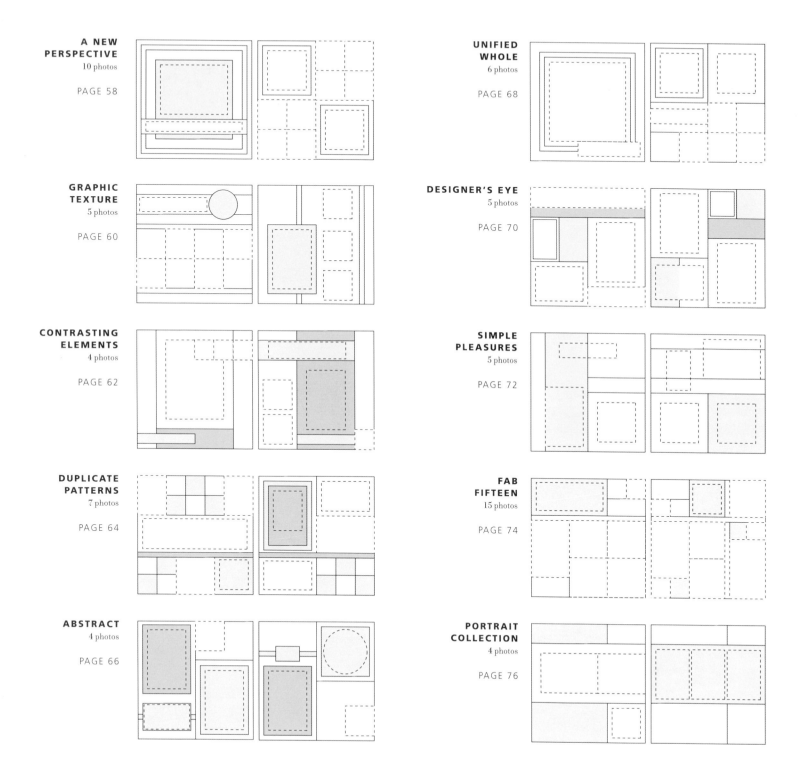

A NEW PERSPECTIVE
10 photos

PAGE 58

GRAPHIC TEXTURE
5 photos

PAGE 60

CONTRASTING ELEMENTS
4 photos

PAGE 62

DUPLICATE PATTERNS
7 photos

PAGE 64

ABSTRACT
4 photos

PAGE 66

UNIFIED WHOLE
6 photos

PAGE 68

DESIGNER'S EYE
5 photos

PAGE 70

SIMPLE PLEASURES
5 photos

PAGE 72

FAB FIFTEEN
15 photos

PAGE 74

PORTRAIT COLLECTION
4 photos

PAGE 76

© 2005 JRL PUBLICATIONS

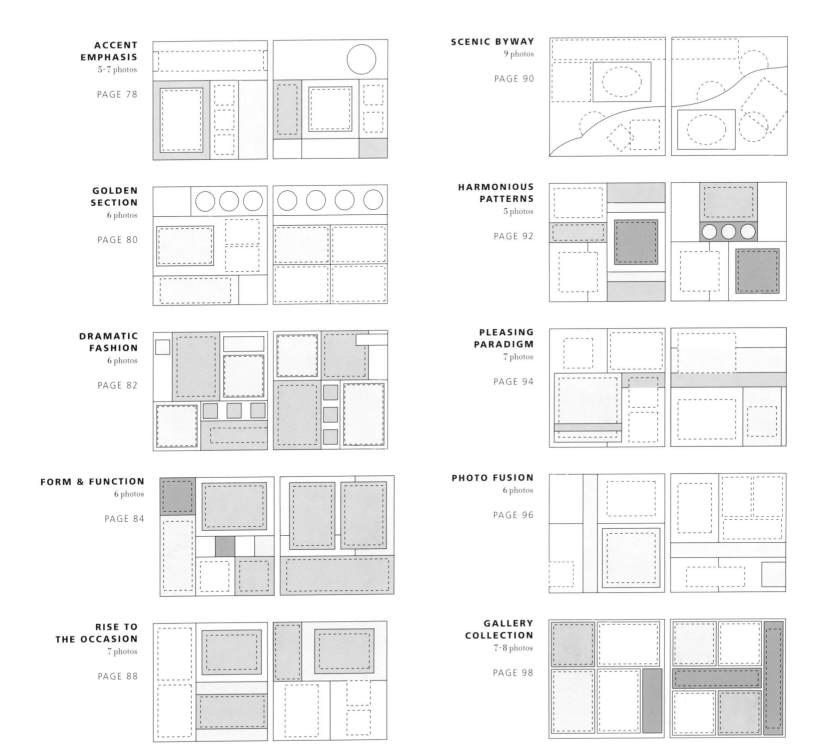

ACCENT EMPHASIS
5-7 photos

PAGE 78

GOLDEN SECTION
6 photos

PAGE 80

DRAMATIC FASHION
6 photos

PAGE 82

FORM & FUNCTION
6 photos

PAGE 84

RISE TO THE OCCASION
7 photos

PAGE 88

SCENIC BYWAY
9 photos

PAGE 90

HARMONIOUS PATTERNS
5 photos

PAGE 92

PLEASING PARADIGM
7 photos

PAGE 94

PHOTO FUSION
6 photos

PAGE 96

GALLERY COLLECTION
7-8 photos

PAGE 98

© 2005 JRL PUBLICATIONS

Quick Reference

THEN & NOW
5 photos

PAGE 100

CLEAR DIMENSION
6 photos

PAGE 102

BALANCED BLOCKS
2–5 photos

PAGE 104

EASY INSPIRATION
7 photos

PAGE 106

RISE 'N SHINE
6 photos

PAGE 108

TREASURE TAGS
5 photos

PAGE 110

PUZZLE JUNKIE
5 photos

PAGE 112

WINNING LAYOUT
6 photos

PAGE 114

DYNAMIC DESIGN
5 photos

PAGE 116

GIVE ME TEN
5 photos

PAGE 118

© 2005 JRL PUBLICATIONS

embrace

"SCRAPBOOKS ARE CONNECTIONS TO THE HANDS
WE HOLD AND THE HANDS THAT HOLD US."

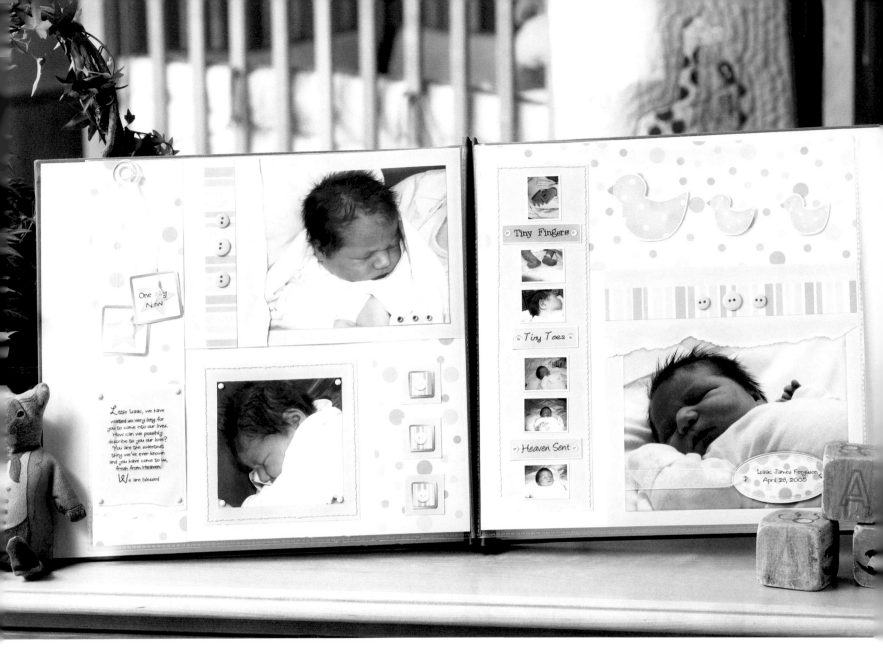

ELEGANT CONTEXT **KEEP THINGS IN CONTEXT WITH SMALL ACCENTS AND LARGE PHOTOS**

Cutting Instructions

B&T Paper

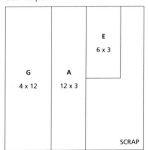

G
4 x 12

A
12 x 3

E
6 x 3

SCRAP

Cardstock*

H
11 x 3

I
11 x 8

SCRAP

Cardstock*

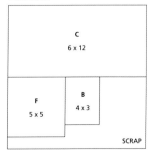

C
6 x 12

F
5 x 5

B
4 x 3

SCRAP

B&T Paper

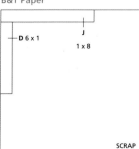

D 6 x 1

J
1 x 8

SCRAP

*Identical papers

© 2005 JRL PUBLICATIONS

Layout Materials

12" x 12" Base Cardstock (2)
12" x 12" Cardstock (2)
12" x 12" B&T Paper (2)

Left Page Dimensions

A 12" x 3"
B 4" x 3"
C 6" x 12"
D 6" x 1"
E 6" x 3"
F 5" x 5"

Right Page Dimensions

G 4" x 12"
H 11" x 3"
I 11" x 8"
J 1" x 8"

Photo Suggestions

1 5" x 7"
2 4" x 4"
3 7" x 7"

Suggested Title

1 10" x 2-1/2"

Suggested Journaling

1 3" x 2-1/2"

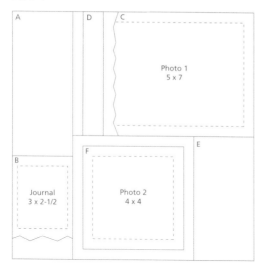

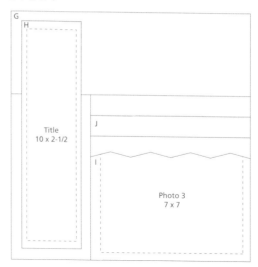

1 Using one 12" x 12" cardstock as your base, attach piece A to the left side of the page, keeping the edges flush.

2 Attach piece B to the bottom of piece A, placing it 1" up from the bottom, keeping the edges flush.

3 Leaving a 9" base, fold the torn left end of piece C over approximately 2-1/2" (the piece will fit the area across the top of the page). Fold flat, adhering only on the top and bottom in order to place the photo inside the fold. Attach to the page, keeping the edges flush.

4 Attach piece D to the top flap of piece C as shown.

5 Attach piece E to the bottom right corner of the page, keeping the edges flush.

6 Attach piece F to the center of the exposed base on the bottom of the page, placing it approximately 1/2" from the bottom edge and other pieces.

7 Attach the specified photos (photos 1-2) to the appropriate areas, centering them on the mats.

1 Using one 12" x 12" cardstock as your base, attach piece G to the top of the page, keeping the edges flush.

2 Attach piece H to the left side of the page, placing it 1/2" from the top and 1/2" from the left edge.

3 Leaving an 8" base, fold the torn top end of piece I over approximately 2-1/2" (the piece will fill the bottom right corner of the page). Fold flat, adhering only on the sides in order to place a photo inside the fold. Attach to the page, keeping the edges flush.

4 Attach piece J to the top flap of piece I as shown.

5 Attach the specified photo (photo 3) to the appropriate areas.

Tip & Technique
Chalking

Journaling Idea
Accentuate a title
with small photos.

*For full recipe and Tip &
Technique see index pg. 120*

© 2005 JRL PUBLICATIONS

Asymmetric

Layout Materials

12" x 12" Base Cardstock (2)
12" x 12" B&T Paper (3)

Left Page Dimensions

A 3" x 3"
B 9" x 3"
C 12" x 1"
D 4-1/2" x 4"
E 6" x 8"

Right Page Dimensions

F 10-1/2" x 8"
G 3" x 2-1/2"
H 7" x 3"
I 1" x 12"

Photo Suggestions

1 4" x 6" (2)
2 3" x 3" (2)
3 4" x 3 1/2"

Suggested Title

1 1-1/2" x 8"

Suggested Journaling

1 6-1/2" x 2-1/2"

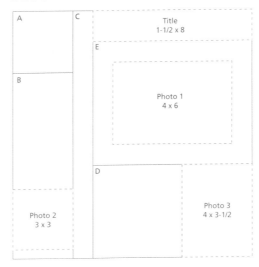

LEFT

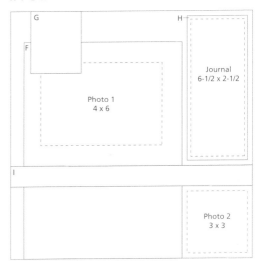

RIGHT

1 Using one 12" x 12" cardstock as your base, attach piece A to the top left corner of the page, keeping the edges flush.

2 Attach piece B under piece A, keeping the left edge flush.

3 Attach piece C down the page, placing it 3" from the left edge next to pieces A and B, and keeping the top and bottom edges flush.

4 Attach piece D to the right of piece C at the bottom of the page, keeping the bottom edges flush.

5 Attach piece E to the right side of the page, placing it flush with the right edge of piece C and the top edge of piece D.

6 Attach the specified photos (photos 1-3) to the appropriate areas, centering them on the mats.

1 Using one 12" x 12" cardstock as your base, attach piece F to the left side, placing it 1/2" from the left and keeping the bottom edge flush.

2 Attach piece G over the top of piece F, placing it 1" from the left and keeping the top edges flush. Adhere on the top edge so photo can slip under the bottom edge.

3 Attach piece H to the right side of the page, placing it 1/4" from the top and right edges.

4 Attach piece I 1/4" below piece H, keeping the edges flush.

5 Attach the specified photos (photos 1-2) to the appropriate areas, centering them on the mats.

Tip & Technique
Antiquing paper

Journaling Idea
Journal directly on the mat and eliminate the journaling box.

For full recipe and Tip & Technique see index pg. 120

© 2005 JRL PUBLICATIONS

Cutting Instructions

B&T Paper

B 9 x 3	**E** 6 x 8	**H** 7 x 3
G 3 x 2-1/2		SCRAP

B&T Paper

F 10-1/2 x 8	**D** 4-1/2 x 4
	A 3 x 3
	SCRAP

B&T Paper

C 12 x 1

I 1 x 12

SCRAP

© 2005 JRL PUBLICATIONS

SILVER SCREEN MAKE YOUR MEMORIES SHINE LIKE A MOVIE ON THE SILVER SCREEN

.... *Cutting Instructions* ....

Cardstock

| I |
| 4 x 12 |

| D |
| 2 x 12 |

M 1/2 x 12   **G** 1/2 x 6
C 1/2 x 4

SCRAP

B&T Paper

| A | L |
| 6 x 8 | 7 x 6 |

| E | |
| 4 x 3 | |

SCRAP

B&T Paper

| K |
| 7 x 6 |

| F |
| 4 x 3 |

SCRAP

Cardstock

J	B
3 x 3	5 x 4
J	
3 x 3	
J	H 1-1/4" Circle
3 x 3	N 1-1/4" Circle

SCRAP

© 2005 JRL PUBLICATIONS

Layout Materials

12" x 12" Base Cardstock (2)
12" x 12" Cardstock (2)
12" x 12" B&T Paper (2)

Left Page Dimensions

A 6" x 8"
B 5" x 4"
C 1/2" x 4"
D 2" x 12"
E 4" x 3"
F 4" x 3"
G 1/2" x 6"
H 1-1/4" circle

Right Page Dimensions

I 4" x 12"
J 3" x 3" (3)
K 7" x 6"
L 7" x 6"
M 1/2" x 12"
N 1-1/4" circle

Photo Suggestions

1 4" x 5"
2 3" x 3"
3 5" x 4" (2)
4 2-1/2" x 2-1/2" (3)

Suggested Title

1 1-1/2" x 11-1/2"

Suggested Journaling

1 3-1/2" x 5-1/2"

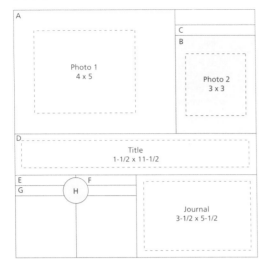

Photo 1
4 x 5

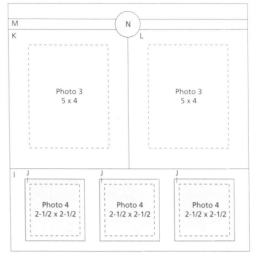

Photo 2
3 x 3

Title
1-1/2 x 11-1/2

H

Journal
3-1/2 x 5-1/2

N

Photo 3
5 x 4

Photo 3
5 x 4

Photo 4
2-1/2 x 2-1/2

Photo 4
2-1/2 x 2-1/2

Photo 4
2-1/2 x 2-1/2

1 Using one 12" x 12" cardstock as your base, attach piece A to the top left side of the page, keeping the edges flush.

2 Attach piece B to the right side of the page 1" from the top, keeping the edges flush.

3 Attach piece C to the top of piece B, keeping the edges flush.

4 Attach piece D directly below pieces A and B, keeping the edges flush.

5 Attach piece E to the bottom left corner of the page, keeping the edges flush.

6 Attach piece F to the bottom, directly next to piece E, keeping the edges flush.

7 Attach piece G on the top of pieces E and F, 1/2" from the top edges, keeping the left edges flush.

8 Attach piece H directly on piece G and the intersection of pieces E and F.

9 Attach the specified photos (photos 1-2) to the appropriate areas, centering them on the mats.

1 Using one 12" x 12" cardstock as your base, attach piece I to the bottom of the page, keeping the edges flush.

2 Attach three pieces J, centered horizontally, to piece I, 1/2" from the top and bottom edges, spacing them 1" apart.

3 Attach piece K to the left side of the page, directly above piece I, keeping the edges flush.

4 Attach piece L to the right side of the page, directly above piece I and next to piece K, keeping the edges flush.

5 Attach piece M directly above pieces K and L, keeping the edges flush.

6 Attach piece N directly on piece M and the intersection of pieces K and L.

7 Attach the specified photos (photos 3-4) to the appropriate areas, centering them on the mats.

Tip & Technique
Crinkled vellum

Journaling Idea
Coordinate the ink colors for your title & journaling with the colors of your page.

For full recipe and Tip & Technique see index pg. 120

© 2005 JRL PUBLICATIONS

Filling Spaces

Layout Materials

12" x 12" Base Cardstock (2)
12" x 12" Cardstock (3)
12" x 12" B&T Paper (2)

Left Page Dimensions

A 9" x 9"
B 8" x 6"
C 1" x 9"
D 9" x 3"
E 4" x 3"
F 3" x 9"
G 3" x 3"

Right Page Dimensions

H 12" x 3"
I 3" x 9"
J 6" x 9"
K 3" x 9"
L 8" x 6"
M 3" x 3" (3)

Photo Suggestions

1 7" x 5" (2)
2 3-1/2" x 2-1/2"
3 2-1/2" x 2-1/2" (3)

Suggested Title

1 2-1/4" x 4-1/2"

Suggested Journaling

1 2-1/2" x 8-1/2"

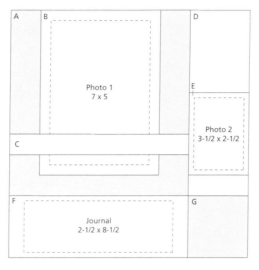

Photo 1
7 x 5

Photo 2
3-1/2 x 2-1/2

Journal
2-1/2 x 8-1/2

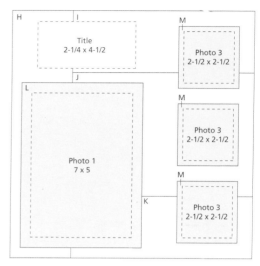

Title
2-1/4 x 4-1/2

Photo 3
2-1/2 x 2-1/2

Photo 3
2-1/2 x 2-1/2

Photo 1
7 x 5

Photo 3
2-1/2 x 2-1/2

1 Using one 12" x 12" cardstock as your base, attach piece A to the top left corner of the page, keeping the edges flush.

2 Attach piece B to piece A, placing it 1-1/2" from the left and keeping the top edge flush.

3 Attach piece C to the bottom of pieces A and B, placing it 6" down from the top. Attach only on the ends so that the photo can be carefully slipped underneath.

4 Attach piece D to the right of pieces A and C, keeping the edges flush.

5 Attach piece E onto piece D, 1" from the bottom edge, keeping the side edges flush.

6 Attach piece F to the bottom left corner of the page, keeping the edges flush.

7 Attach piece G to the bottom right corner, keeping the edges flush.

8 Attach the specified photos (photos 1-2) to the appropriate areas, centering them on the mats.

1 Using one 12" x 12" cardstock as your base, attach piece H to the top left corner of the page, keeping the edges flush.

2 Attach piece I to the top right corner of the page, keeping the edges flush.

3 Attach piece J directly under piece I, keeping the edges flush.

4 Attach piece K to the bottom right corner of the page, keeping the edges flush.

5 Attach piece L to the bottom left side of the page, placing it 1/2" from left and bottom edges.

6 Attach the piece M mats to the right side of the page, placing them 1-1/4" from the right and 3/4" from the bottom edge and each other.

7 Attach the specified photos (photos 1 and 3) to the appropriate areas, centering them on the mats.

Tip & Technique
Paper leather

Journaling Idea
Use the large journaling square if you have a long story to tell. If not, use it for a title.

For full recipe and Tip & Technique see index pg. 120

© 2005 JRL PUBLICATIONS

Howdy

My little boys have always idolized my Dad. And what's not to idolize? Perhaps they've learned their admiration from me. My Dad is hard working, honest, trustworthy, and his quiet manner makes all who know him respect his ways. So when the boys got the chance to wear Gump's boots and hat at the cabin one afternoon, they felt pride in who they are and in who they have the potential to become. And so did I. These are definitely some big boots to fill, but my Dad is one cowboy I want my boys to strive to become.

FILLING SPACES PATTERNS AND TEXTURES FILL SPACES AROUND THESE PHOTOS

Cutting Instructions

B&T Paper

F 3 x 9	
I 3 x 9	D 9 x 3
K 3 x 9	
	SCRAP

B&T Paper

B 8 x 6
H 12 x 3
SCRAP

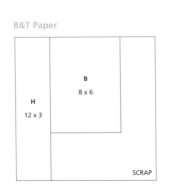

Cardstock

J 6 x 9	E 4 x 3
C 1 x 9	
	SCRAP

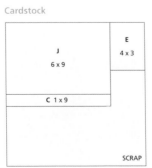

Cardstock*

A 9 x 9	G 3 x 3
	M 3 x 3
	M 3 x 3
SCRAP	M 3 x 3

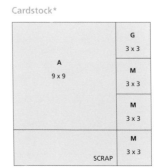

Cardstock*

L 8 x 6
SCRAP

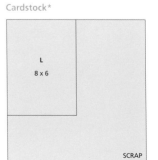

© 2005 JRL PUBLICATIONS

*Identical papers

Cutting Instructions

B&T Paper

C 7 x 7	
H 5 x 5	SCRAP

B&T Paper

E 7 x 5	
F 5 x 7	SCRAP

Cardstock

G 7 x 7	
A 5 x 7	SCRAP

B&T Paper

I 7 x 5	
B 5 x 5	SCRAP

Cardstock

J 11 x 4	**D** 5-1/2 x 5-1/2
	SCRAP

© 2005 JRL PUBLICATIONS

LEFT

RIGHT

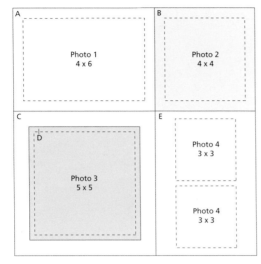

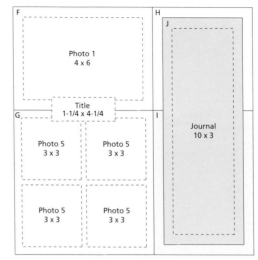

Layout Materials

12" x 12" Base Cardstock (2)
12" x 12" Cardstock (2)
12" x 12" B&T Paper (3)

*Left Page
Dimensions*

A 5" x 7"
B 5" x 5"
C 7" x 7"
D 5-1/2" x 5-1/2"
E 7" x 5"

*Right Page
Dimensions*

F 5" x 7"
G 7" x 7"
H 5" x 5"
I 7" x 5"
J 11" x 4"

*Photo
Suggestions*

1 4" x 6" (2)
2 4" x 4"
3 5" x 5"
4 3" x 3" (2) or 6" x 4"
5 3" x 3" (4)

Suggested Title

1 1-1/4" x 4-1/4"

*Suggested
Journaling*

1 10" x 3"

1 Using one sheet of 12" x 12" cardstock as your base, attach piece A to the top left corner of the page, keeping the edges flush.

2 Attach piece B to the top right corner of the page, keeping the edges flush.

3 Attach piece C to the bottom left corner of the page, keeping the edges flush.

4 Attach piece D to the center of piece C, placing it 3/4" from the edges.

5 Attach piece E to the bottom right corner of the page, keeping the edges flush.

6 Attach the specified photos (photos 1-4) to the appropriate areas, centering them on the mats.

1 Using one 12" x 12" cardstock as your base, attach piece F to the top left corner of the page, keeping the edges flush.

2 Attach piece G to the bottom left corner of the page, keeping the edges flush.

3 Attach piece H to the top right corner of the page, keeping the edges flush.

4 Attach piece I to the bottom right corner of the page, keeping the edges flush.

5 Attach piece J to the center of pieces H and I, placing it 1/2" from the edges.

6 Attach the specified photos (photos 1 and 5) to the appropriate areas, centering them on the mats.

Tip & Technique
Chalk popping

Journaling Idea
**Be creative with
journaling space by
dressing things up.**

*For full recipe and Tip &
Technique see index pg. 121*

© 2005 JRL PUBLICATIONS

Column Composition

Layout Materials

12" x 12" Base Cardstock (2)
12" x 12" Cardstock (3)
12" x 12" B&T Paper (2)

Left Page Dimensions

A 12" x 5-1/2"
B 12" x 3"
C 12" x 3-1/2"
D 6-1/2" x 4-1/2"
E 2" x 2" (4)

Right Page Dimensions

F 8-1/2" x 6"
G 1-1/2" x 3-1/2"
H 5" x 5"
I 2" x 6"
J 1" x 6"
K 6-1/2" x 6"
L 5" x 5"
M 3-1/2" x 12"
N 1-1/2" x 12"
O 1/2" x 12"
P 2" x 2" (3)

Photo Suggestions

1 6" x 4"
2 4" x 4" (2)

Suggested Title

1 2-1/2" x 4-1/2"

Suggested Journaling

1 10" x 2-1/2"

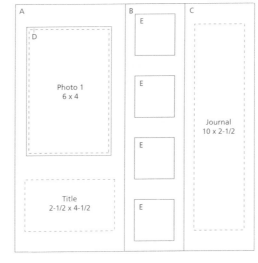

Left page diagram:
- A
- B / E
- C
- D
- Photo 1 6 x 4
- Journal 10 x 2-1/2
- Title 2-1/2 x 4-1/2

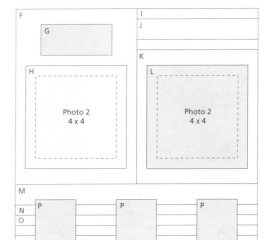

Right page diagram:
- F
- G
- I
- J
- H
- K
- Photo 2 4 x 4
- L
- Photo 2 4 x 4
- M
- N
- O
- P P P

1 Using one 12" x 12" cardstock as your base, attach piece A to the left of the page, keeping the edges flush.

2 Attach piece B to the right of piece A, keeping the edges flush.

3 Attach piece C along the right side of piece B, keeping the edges flush.

4 Attach piece D, centered side-to-side, onto piece A, 1-1/4" from the top of the page.

5 Starting 1/2" from the top of piece B, center the four pieces E, 1" apart, leaving 1/2" at the bottom of the page.

6 Attach the specified photo (photo 1) to the appropriate area, centering it on the mat.

1 Using one 12" x 12" cardstock as your base, attach piece F to the top left corner of the page, keeping the edges flush.

2 Attach piece G to the top center of piece F, 3/4" from the top edge.

3 Attach piece H to the center of piece F, 1/2" below piece G.

4 Attach piece I to the top right corner of the page, keeping edges flush.

5 Attach piece J to the center of piece I, keeping the left edges flush.

6 Attach piece K below piece I, keeping the right edges flush.

7 Attach piece L to piece K, 3/4" from the top and bottom edge and 1/2" from the right and left edge.

8 Attach piece M to the bottom of the page, keeping the edges flush.

9 Attach piece N to the center of piece M, keeping the edges flush.

10 Attach piece O to the center of piece N, keeping the edges flush.

11 Attach the three pieces P onto pieces N and O, placing them 1-1/2" from the side edges and 1-1/2" from each other.

12 Attach the specified photos (photos 2) to the appropriate areas, centering them on the mats.

Tip & Technique
Highlight journaling with chalk

Journaling Idea
Create a fun title by alternating different fonts.

For full recipe and Tip & Technique see index pg. 121

© 2005 JRL PUBLICATIONS

COLUMN COMPOSITION CREATE COMPOSITION BASED ON THE SIMPLE PRINCIPLE OF COLUMNS

·········· *Cutting Instructions* ··································

B&T Paper

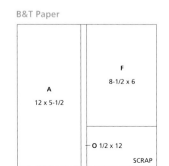

A
12 x 5-1/2

F
8-1/2 x 6

O 1/2 x 12

SCRAP

B&T Paper

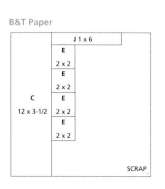

J 1 x 6

E
2 x 2

E
2 x 2

C
12 x 3-1/2

E
2 x 2

E
2 x 2

SCRAP

Cardstock

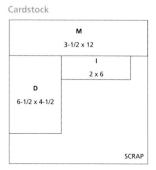

M
3-1/2 x 12

I
2 x 6

D
6-1/2 x 4-1/2

SCRAP

Cardstock

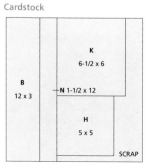

K
6-1/2 x 6

B
12 x 3

N 1-1/2 x 12

H
5 x 5

SCRAP

Cardstock

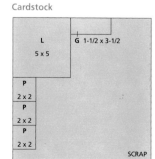

L
5 x 5

G 1-1/2 x 3-1/2

P
2 x 2

P
2 x 2

P
2 x 2

SCRAP

© 2005 JRL PUBLICATIONS

.... *Cutting Instructions* ....

B&T Paper

I 12 x 6	**B** 9 x 3
	M 1 x 10
	G 1 x 12
	SCRAP

B&T Paper

K 12 x 2	**A** 9 x 3
	SCRAP

B&T Paper

J 12 x 4	**C** 9 x 6
	SCRAP

Cardstock

E 3 x 12
SCRAP

Cardstock*

F 1-1/2 x 12
L 1-1/2 x 10
O 4-1/2 x 6-1/2
O 4-1/2 x 6-1/2
N 2-1/2 x 2-1/2
H 2-1/2 x 2-1/2
SCRAP

*Identical papers

© 2005 JRL PUBLICATIONS

Layout Materials

12" x 12" Base Cardstock (2)
12" x 12" Cardstock (3)
12" x 12" B&T Paper (3)

Left Page Dimensions

A 9" x 3"
B 9" x 3"
C 9" x 6"
D 8" x 6"
E 3" x 12"
F 1-1/2" x 12"
G 1" x 12"
H 2-1/2" x 2-1/2"

Right Page Dimensions

I 12" x 6"
J 12" x 4"
K 12" x 2"
L 1-1/2" x 10"
M 1" x 10"
N 2-1/2" x 2-1/2"
O 4-1/2" x 6-1/2" (2)

Photo Suggestions

1 6" x 5"
2 2" x 2" (2)
3 4" x 6"

Suggested Title

1 1-1/2" x 6"

Suggested Journaling

1 4" x 6"

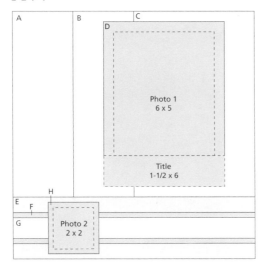

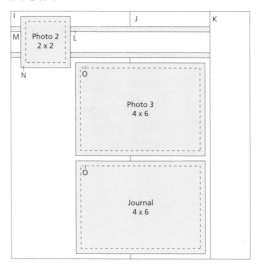

1 Using one 12" x 12" cardstock as your base, attach piece A to the top left corner of the page, keeping the edges flush.

2 Attach piece B directly to the right of piece A, keeping the edges flush.

3 Attach piece C to the top right corner of the page, keeping the edges flush.

4 Attach piece D to the page, placing it 1/2" from the top and 1-1/2" from the right edge.

5 Attach piece E to the bottom of the page, keeping the edges flush.

6 Attach piece F to the center of piece E, keeping the side edges flush.

7 Attach piece G to the center of piece F, keeping the side edges flush.

8 Attach piece H to the bottom left corner, placing it 1-3/4" from the left and 1/4" from the bottom edge of the page.

9 Attach the specified photos (photos 1-2) to the appropriate areas, centering them on the mats.

1 Using one 12" x 12" cardstock as your base, attach piece I to the left side of the page, keeping the edges flush.

2 Attach piece J directly to the right of piece I, keeping the edges flush.

3 Attach piece K to the right side of the page, keeping the edges flush.

4 Attach piece L to the top of the page, placing it 1" down from the top and directly to the left of piece K.

5 Attach piece M to the center of piece L, keeping the side edges flush.

6 Attach piece N to the left side of pieces L and M, placing it 5/8" from the left and 3/8" from the top edges.

7 Attach the two piece O mats to the page, placing them 3-1/4" from the left and 1/4" from the bottom edge and from each other.

8 Attach the specified photos (photos 2-3) to the appropriate areas, centering them on the mats.

Cardstock*

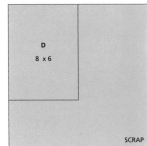

Tip & Technique
Liquid Appliqué™

Journaling Idea
Create a title
using tags.

For full recipe and Tip & Technique see index pg. 121

© 2005 JRL PUBLICATIONS

Simple Contrast

Layout Materials

12" x 12" Base Cardstock (2)
12" x 12" Cardstock (2)
12" x 12" B&T Paper (2)

Left Page Dimensions

A 4" x 12"
B 1/2" x 12"
C 4" x 4"
D 4" x 4"
E 8" x 4"

Right Page Dimensions

F 4" x 4"
G 1/2" x 4"
H 4" x 8"
I 2" x 2"
J 8" x 4"
K 7" x 7"

Photo Suggestions

1 3" x 3" (5)
2 6" x 6"

Suggested Title

1 2" x 8-1/2"

Suggested Journaling

1 7" x 3"

LEFT

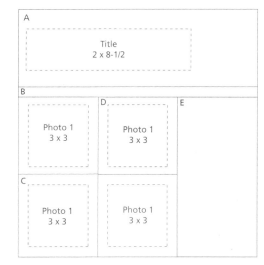

A — Title 2 x 8-1/2
B
C — Photo 1 3 x 3
D — Photo 1 3 x 3
E
Photo 1 3 x 3
Photo 1 3 x 3

RIGHT

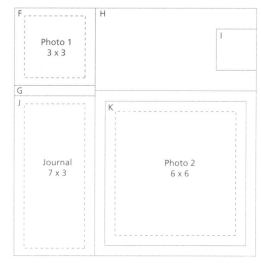

F — Photo 1 3 x 3
H
I
G
J — Journal 7 x 3
K — Photo 2 6 x 6

LEFT

1 Using one 12" x 12" cardstock as your base, attach piece A to the top of the page, keeping the edges flush.

2 Attach piece B to the bottom of piece A, keeping the edges flush.

3 Attach piece C to the bottom left corner of the page, keeping the edges flush.

4 Attach piece D to the page directly under pieces A and B and 4" from the side edges.

5 Attach piece E to the right side of the page, keeping the edges flush.

6 Attach the specified photos (photos 1) to the appropriate areas, centering them on the mats.

RIGHT

1 Using one 12" x 12" cardstock as your base, attach piece F to the top left corner of the page, keeping the edges flush.

2 Attach piece G to the bottom of piece F, keeping the edges flush. (If completing the two-page layout, be sure to line up the piece B and G strips across the pages.)

3 Attach piece H to the top right corner of the page, keeping the edges flush.

4 Attach piece I to the right edge of piece H, 1" from the top of the page.

5 Attach piece J to the bottom left corner of the page, keeping edges flush.

6 Attach piece K to the bottom right corner of the page, placing it 1/2" from the right and bottom edges.

7 Attach the specified photos (photos 1-2) to the appropriate areas, centering them on the mats.

Tip & Technique
Dimensional Elements

Journaling Idea
Use a poem to express feelings.

For full recipe and Tip & Technique see index pg. 121

© 2005 JRL PUBLICATIONS

When we have grown and move away,
and leave our childhood behind,
Will thoughts of special memories
come often to your mind?

Will you remember giggling,
secrets that we shared,
the pillow fights, and pillow talks,
and things that made us scared?

Or what about our pulling hair,
or braiding it for each other,
will you still remember
all the things we did to our brother

Will all the little memories
hold a special place of their own?
Will the love we have for each other
be the same when we are grown?

Our dreams may change,
and our lives go different directions,
but the miles, and the years,
will not sever our connection.

Always remember that I love you,
think of me now and then,
the only thing that matters,
you're my sister, my best friend.

COLOR CELEBRATION THIS PAGE DESIGN IS GREAT FOR CELEBRATING A NEW COLOR COMBINATION

······ *Cutting Instructions* ·····································

Cardstock

A
4 x 12

J
8 x 4

Cardstock

B 1/2 x 12

G 1/2 x 4

C
4 x 4

K
7 x 7

I
2 x 2

SCRAP

B&T Paper

H
4 x 8

D
4 x 4

SCRAP

B&T Paper

E
8 x 4

F
4 x 4

SCRAP

© 2005 JRL PUBLICATIONS

Back to School

Lay out your clothes, sharpen your pencils, and pack a lunch. It's time to go back to school

Aubrey has been so sad now that Rachel started Kindergarten. We walk her to the bus stop and pick her up after school. Aubrey asks me everyday, "Mom, is it time to go get Rachel?" She also says, "Someday I'll be a big girl and go to school." I cannot believe how fast my girls are growing up.

August 12, 2004

AESTHETIC BALANCE THESE ELEMENTS WORK TOGETHER FOR ATTRACTIVE AESTHETIC BALANCE

.... *Cutting Instructions* ....

B&T Paper

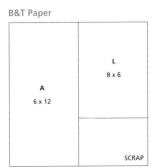

A
6 x 12

L
8 x 6

SCRAP

B&T Paper

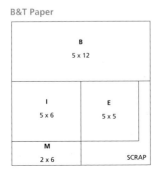

B
5 x 12

I
5 x 6

E
5 x 5

M
2 x 6

SCRAP

Cardstock

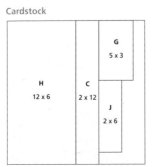

H
12 x 6

C
2 x 12

G
5 x 3

J
2 x 6

Cardstock

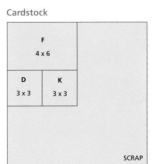

F
4 x 6

D
3 x 3

K
3 x 3

SCRAP

© 2005 JRL PUBLICATIONS

Layout Materials

12" x 12" Base Cardstock (2)
12" x 12" Cardstock (2)
12" x 12" B&T Paper (2)

Left Page Dimensions

A 6" x 12"
B 5" x 12"
C 2" x 12"
D 3" x 3"
E 5" x 5"
F 4" x 6"
G 5" x 3"

Right Page Dimensions

H 12" x 6"
I 5" x 6"
J 2" x 6"
K 3" x 3"
L 8" x 6"
M 2" x 6"

Photo Suggestions

1 3-1/2" x 5-1/2"
2 2-1/2" x 2-1/2" (2)
3 3" x 3" (2)
4 6" x 4"

Suggested Title

1 2-1/2" x 2-1/2"

Suggested Journaling

1 3-1/2" x 6"

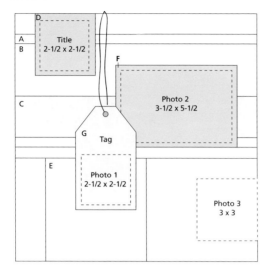

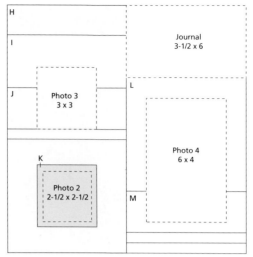

1 Using one 12" x 12" cardstock as your base, attach piece A to the page 1" from the top, keeping side edges flush.

2 Attach piece B onto the center of piece A.

3 Attach piece C to piece B, placing it 1" from the bottom.

4 Attach piece D to the top of the page, placing it 1" from the left corner, keeping the top edges flush.

5 Attach piece E to the bottom of the page, placing it 1-1/2" from the left side, keeping bottom edges flush.

6 Attach piece F to the right side of the page, placing it 2" from the top and 1" from the right.

7 Cut the top corners of piece G diagonally to create a tag.

8 Attach piece G to the page, placing it 2-1/2" from the bottom and 3" from the left edge of the page.

9 Attach 10" piece of ribbon to piece G tag as illustrated if desired.

10 Attach the specified photos (photos 1-3) to the appropriate areas, centering them on the mats.

1 Using one 12" x 12" cardstock as your base, attach piece H to the left side of the page, keeping the edges flush.

2 Attach piece I to piece H, placing it 1-1/2" down from the top, keeping the left edges flush.

3 Attach piece J to piece I, placing it 1" from the bottom.

4 Attach piece K to the bottom of piece H, placing it 1-1/2" from the left and 1-1/4" from the bottom edges.

5 Attach piece L to the right of the page, 3-1/2" down from the top, keeping the right edges flush.

6 Attach piece M to piece L, 1/2" from the bottom.

7 Attach the specified photos (photos 2-4) to the appropriate areas, centering them on the mats.

Tip & Technique
Using marker ink on stamps

Journaling Idea
Use a date as an embellishment.

For full recipe and Tip & Technique see index pg. 121

© 2005 JRL PUBLICATIONS

Layout Materials

12" x 12" Base Cardstock (2)
12" x 12" Base Cardstock (4)
12" x 12" B&T Paper (1)

Left Page Dimensions

A 3" x 6"
B 5" x 6"
C 5" x 1"
D 3-1/2" x 3-1/2"
E 12" x 6"
F 6-1/2" x 4-1/2"
G 4-1/2" x 4-1/2"

Right Page Dimensions

H 7" x 6"
I 6-1/2" x 4-1/2"
J 5" x 6"
K 3-1/2" x 2" (2)
L 12" x 6"
M 4-1/2" x 4-1/2"
N 6-1/2" x 4-1/2"
O 12" x 1"
P 1-1/2" x 1-1/2"

Photo Suggestions

1 4" x 6"
2 6" x 4" (3)
3 4" x 4" (2)

Suggested Title

1 2" x 5-1/2"

Suggested Journaling

1 3" x 3"

LEFT

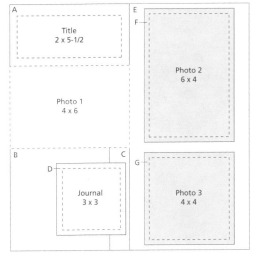

Title
2 x 5-1/2

Photo 1
4 x 6

Photo 2
6 x 4

Journal
3 x 3

Photo 3
4 x 4

RIGHT

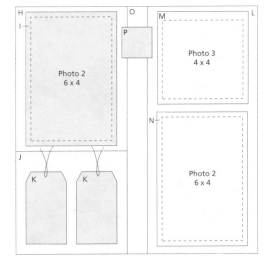

Photo 2
6 x 4

Photo 3
4 x 4

K   K

Photo 2
6 x 4

1 Using one 12" x 12" cardstock as your base, attach piece A to the top left side of the page, keeping the edges flush.

2 Attach piece B to the bottom left corner of the page, keeping the edges flush.

3 Attach piece C to the right side of piece B, keeping the edges flush.

4 Attach piece D to the right side of pieces B and C, placing it 5/8" from the bottom and 1/4" from the right edge.

5 Attach piece E to the right side of the page, keeping the edges flush.

6 Attach piece F to the top of piece E, placing it 3/4" from the right and 1/4" from the top edge.

7 Attach piece G to the bottom of piece E, placing it 3/4" from the right and 1/4" from the bottom edge.

8 Attach the specified photos (photos 1-3) to the appropriate areas, centering them on the mats.

1 Using one 12" x 12" cardstock as your base, attach piece H to the top left side of the page, keeping the edges flush.

2 Attach piece I to the center of piece H, placing it 1/2" from the sides and 1/4" from the top and bottom.

3 Attach piece J to the bottom left corner of the page, keeping the edges flush.

4 Attach the two piece K accents to piece J on the bottom left of the page, arranging as desired. Attach with ribbon if desired.

5 Attach piece L to the right side of the page, keeping the edges flush.

6 Attach piece M to the top of piece L, placing it 1/2" from the right and 1/4" from the top edge of the page.

7 Attach piece N 1/4" below piece M centered side to side onto piece L.

8 Attach piece O down the center of the page over pieces H and L.

9 Attach piece P over piece O, 1" from the top.

10 Attach the specified photos (photos 2-3) to the appropriate areas, centering them on the mats.

Tip & Technique

Add dimension with 3-D Foam Squares

Journaling Idea

Use an alphabet template to cut out the letters in your title.

For full recipe and Tip & Technique see index pg. 121

© 2005 JRL PUBLICATIONS

Cutting Instructions

B&T Paper

E 12 x 6	**H** 7 x 6
	SCRAP

Cardstock

L 12 x 6	**B** 5 x 6
	SCRAP

Cardstock

O 12 x 1
C 5 x 1

SCRAP

Cardstock

N 6-1/2 x 4-1/2	**J** 5 x 6
	A 3 x 6
M 4-1/2 x 4-1/2	**D** 3-1/2 x 3-1/2
	SCRAP

Cardstock

I 6-1/2 x 4-1/2	**F** 6-1/2 x 4-1/2	
		P 1-1/2 x 1-1/2
G 4-1/2 x 4-1/2	**K** 3-1/2 x 2	**K** 3-1/2 x 2
		SCRAP

© 2005 JRL PUBLICATIONS

CREATIVE RHYTHM **COMBINE A MIXTURE OF ELEMENTS FOR PERSONALIZED CREATIVE RHYTHM**

Cutting Instructions

B&T Paper

- G — 3 x 12
- A — 8 x 8
- L — 4 x 4
- SCRAP

B&T Paper

- C — 2 x 4
- E — 4 x 4
- M — 4 x 4
- K — 3 x 4
- SCRAP

B&T Paper

- I 1/2 x 12
- F 1/2 x 8
- SCRAP

Cardstock

- J — 5 x 8
- D — 4 x 4
- SCRAP

Cardstock

- B — 6 x 6
- H 1-1/2 x 4
- N 2-1/2 x 2-1/2
- SCRAP

© 2005 JRL PUBLICATIONS

Layout Materials

12" x 12" Base Cardstock (2)
12" x 12" Cardstock (2)
12" x 12" B&T Paper (3)

Left Page Dimensions

A 8" x 8"
B 6" x 6"
C 2" x 4"
D 4" x 4"
E 4" x 4"
F 1/2" x 8"

Right Page Dimensions

G 3" x 12"
H 1-1/2" x 4"
I 1/2" x 12"
J 5" x 8"
K 3" x 4"
L 4" x 4"
M 4" x 4"
N 2-1/2" x 2-1/2"

Photo Suggestions

1 4" x 4"
2 4" x 5"
3 6" x 4" (2)
4 3-1/2" x 3-1/2" (3)
5 4" x 6"
6 2" x 2"

Suggested Title

1 1" x 6"

Suggested Journaling

1 3-1/2" x 3-1/2"

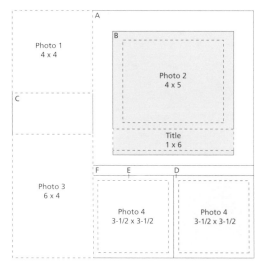

Photo 1
4 x 4

B

Photo 2
4 x 5

C

Title
1 x 6

F E D

Photo 3
6 x 4

Photo 4
3-1/2 x 3-1/2

Photo 4
3-1/2 x 3-1/2

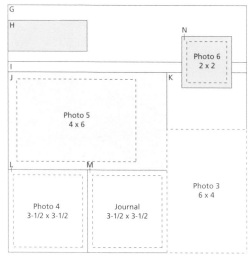

G

H

N

I

Photo 6
2 x 2

J

K

Photo 5
4 x 6

L

M

Photo 3
6 x 4

Photo 4
3-1/2 x 3-1/2

Journal
3-1/2 x 3-1/2

1 Using one 12" x 12" cardstock as your base, attach piece A to the top right corner of the page, keeping the edges flush.

2 Attach piece B to piece A, placing it 1" from the top and 1" from the side edges.

3 Attach piece C to the left side of the page, placing it 4" down from the top and keeping the side edges flush.

4 Attach piece D to the bottom right corner of the page, keeping the edges flush.

5 Attach piece E to the left of piece D, keeping the bottom and right edges flush.

6 Attach piece F to the bottom of piece A, keeping the side edges flush.

7 Attach the specified photos (photos 1-4) to the appropriate areas, centering them on the mats.

1 Using one 12" x 12" cardstock as your base, attach piece G to the top of the page, keeping the edges flush.

2 Attach piece H to the left side of piece G, placing it 1/2" from the top, keeping the left edges flush.

3 Attach piece I onto the bottom of piece G, keeping the side edges flush.

4 Attach piece J to the left side of the page, placing it under piece I, keeping the side edges flush.

5 Attach piece K to the right side of the page, placing it under piece I, keeping the side edges flush.

6 Attach piece L to the bottom left corner of the page, keeping the edges flush.

7 Attach piece M to the right of piece L, keeping the side edges flush.

8 Attach piece N onto piece I, placing it 3/4" from the right edge and 1-1/2" from top edge of the page.

9 Attach the specified photos (photos 3-6) to the appropriate areas, centering them on the mats.

Creative Rhythm

Tip & Technique
Tinting photos with ink

Journaling Idea
Attach vellum sentiments to different areas for added emotion.

For full recipe and Tip & Technique see index pg. 122

© 2005 JRL PUBLICATIONS

Harmony

Layout Materials

12" x 12" Base Cardstock (2)
12" x 12" Cardstock (1)
12" x 12" B&T Paper (3)

Left Page Dimensions

A   12" x 8"
B   3" x 8"
C   1-1/2" circle
D   6-1/2" x 4-1/2"
E   2" x 2"
F   1/2" x 12" (2)

Right Page Dimensions

G   7" x 12"
H   1/2" x 12"
I   1-1/2" circle
J   2" x 2" (2)

Photo Suggestions

1   6" x 4"
2   4" x 4" (2)

Suggested Title/Journaling

1   5" x 8"

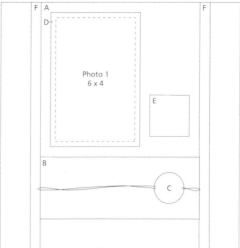

Photo 1
6 x 4

E

B

C

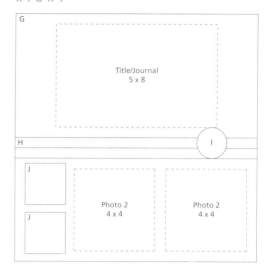

G

Title/Journal
5 x 8

H

I

J

J

Photo 2
4 x 4

Photo 2
4 x 4

Left

1   Using one 12" x 12" cardstock as your base, attach piece A down the center of the page, placing it 2" from the side edges, keeping the top and bottom edges flush.

2   Attach piece B to the bottom of piece A, placing it 1-1/2" from the bottom.

Tip: Consider whether you will wrap a portion of the page in ribbon or an accessory and plan accordingly. You may create a longer piece B to wrap around piece A. Or, you may wrap only piece B before attaching it to piece A, depending on the look you wish to achieve.

3   Attach piece C to ribbon or trim as desired.

4   Attach piece D to piece A, placing it 1/2" down from the top and 1/2" from the left edge of piece A.

5   Attach piece E to the right side of piece A, placing it 4-1/2" down and 2-1/2" from the right edge.

6   Attach pieces F down both sides of piece A, keeping the edges flush.

7   Attach the specified photo (photo 1) to the appropriate area, centering it on the mat.

Right

1   Using one 12" x 12" cardstock as your base, attach piece G to the top of the page, keeping the edges flush.

2   Attach piece H to the bottom of piece G, placing it 1/2" from the bottom edge.

3   Attach piece I to the right side of piece H, placing it 1-1/2" from the right side.

4   Arrange the two piece J squares in the bottom left corner of the page, centered on the exposed base and attach.

5   Attach the specified photos (photos 2) to the appropriate area, as shown.

Tip & Technique
Accenting
with hemp

Journaling Idea
Emphasize part of
your journaling
by repeating one
word & varying the
size and font.

For full recipe and Tip & Technique see index pg. 122

© 2005 JRL PUBLICATIONS

When Grandpa gave Logan exactly what he WANTED (a cowboy hat and boots) for his sixth birthday, Logan was elated. The minute he opened that gift he took possession of the hat and boots as if he'd owned them for years. Now he rarely goes without them. He wears the boots with everything: shorts, swimming suit, Halloween costume, everything! His favorite thing to do in his boots is run through the dirt, kicking dust everywhere. Mom kept getting mad at Logan, telling him he was going to ruin his new boots until finally she asked him why he likes to run through the dirt with them on. Logan replied, "Because my boots make me run so fast, mom. Watch the smoke behind me when I run!" Now mom lets him run in the dirt all he wants with

those boots on because he is just what she has always WANTED as well!

WANTED

cutest kid in the West

HARMONY REPEATING ACCENTS OF THE SAME SIZE CREATES HARMONY

.... *Cutting Instructions* ....

B&T Paper*

A

12 x 8

SCRAP

B&T Paper*

G

7 x 12

SCRAP

Cardstock

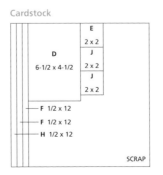

	E
	2 x 2
D	J
6-1/2 x 4-1/2	2 x 2
	J
	2 x 2

F 1/2 x 12
F 1/2 x 12
H 1/2 x 12

SCRAP

B&T Paper

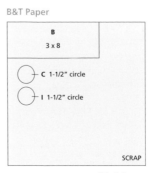

B

3 x 8

C 1-1/2" circle

I 1-1/2" circle

SCRAP

© 2005 JRL PUBLICATIONS

*Identical papers

Cutting Instructions

B&T Paper

F 12 x 2-1/2	F 12 x 2-1/2	D 3 x 8
		C 4 x 4
		SCRAP

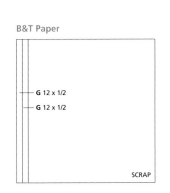

B&T Paper

G 12 x 1/2
G 12 x 1/2

SCRAP

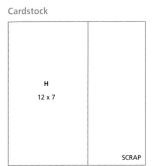

Cardstock

H 12 x 7
SCRAP

Cardstock

E 4-1/2 x 6-1/2	A 4 x 4
E 4-1/2 x 6-1/2	A 4 x 4
	SCRAP

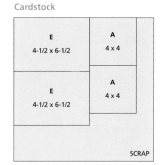

Cardstock

I 5 x 6	I 5 x 6
B 3-1/2 x 3-1/2	J 1 x 1
	SCRAP

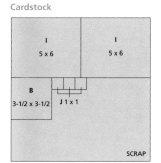

© 2005 JRL PUBLICATIONS

Layout Materials

12" x 12" Base Cardstock (2)
12" x 12" Cardstock (3)
12" x 12" B&T Paper (2)

Left Page Dimensions

A 4" x 4" (2)
B 3-1/2" x 3-1/2"
C 4" x 4"
D 3" x 8"
E 4-1/2" x 6-1/2" (2)

Right Page Dimensions

F 12" x 2-1/2" (2)
G 12" x 1/2" (2)
H 12" x 7"
I 5" x 6" (2)
J 1" x 1" (3)

Photo Suggestions

1 3" x 3"
2 3-1/2" x 3-1/2"
3 4" x 6" (4)

Suggested Title

1 1" x 8"

Suggested Journaling

1 3" x 3"

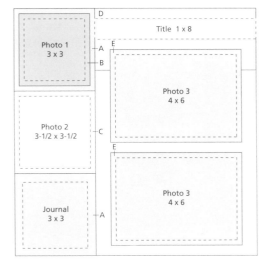

Title 1 x 8

Photo 1
3 x 3

Photo 3
4 x 6

Photo 2
3-1/2 x 3-1/2

Photo 3
4 x 6

Journal
3 x 3

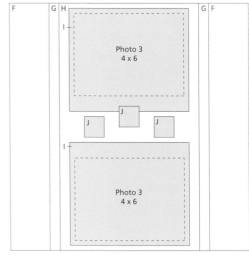

Photo 3
4 x 6

Photo 3
4 x 6

LEFT

1 Using one 12" x 12" cardstock as your base, attach pieces A to the top and bottom left side corners of the page, keeping the edges flush.

2 Attach piece B to the center of top piece A, placing it 1/2" from the top and left edges.

3 Attach piece C between the two pieces A, keeping the edges flush.

4 Attach piece D to the top right corner of the page, keeping the edges flush.

5 Attach both piece E mats to the right side of the page, placing them 2" down from the top edge, 3/4" from the right, and 1/2" from each other.

6 Attach the specified photos (photos 1-3) to the appropriate areas, centering them on the mats.

RIGHT

1 Using one 12" x 12" cardstock as your base, attach one piece F to each side of the page, keeping the edges flush.

2 Attach one piece G to the inside of each piece F, 2" from the edge of the page, keeping the top and bottom edges flush.

3 Attach piece H to the middle of the page, keeping the top and bottom edges flush.

4 Attach the two piece I mats to the center of piece H, 1/4" from the top and bottom edges of the page.

5 Arrange 3 pieces J to middle of H as shown.

6 Attach the specified photos (photos 3) to the appropriate areas, centering them on the mats.

Tip & Technique
Using photos with
a letter template

Journaling Idea
Use the title
block as a
border behind
cut-out lettering.

For full recipe and Tip & Technique see index pg. 122

© 2005 JRL PUBLICATIONS

Layout Materials

12" x 12" Base Cardstock (2)
12" x 12" Cardstock (2)
12" x 12" B&T Paper (2)

Left Page Dimensions

A 8" x 8"
B 1" x 12"
C 4" x 8"
D 6-1/2" x 4-1/2"

Right Page Dimensions

E 8" x 4"
F 8" x 4"
G 1" x 12"

Photo Suggestions

1 6" x 4"
2 4" x 6" (2)

Suggested Title

1 2" x 3"

Suggested Journaling

1 2" x 4-1/2"
2 4-1/2" x 2"

LEFT

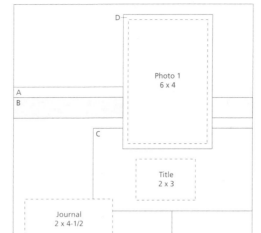

RIGHT

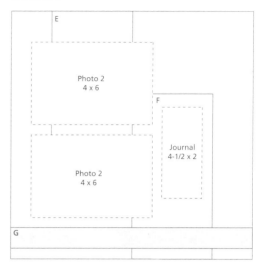

1 Using one 12" x 12" cardstock as your base, attach piece A to the bottom left corner of the page, keeping the edges flush.

2 Trim piece B as desired. (Ours is cut on a slight angle.) Attach piece B across the page, on top of piece A, placing it approximately 4-1/2" down from the top.

3 Attach piece C to the right side of the page, placing it 2" from the bottom, keeping the right edges flush.

4 Attach piece D to the page, placing it 1/2" from the top and 2" from right edge of the page.

5 Attach the specified photo (photo 1) to the appropriate area, centering it on the mat.

1 Using one 12" x 12" cardstock as your base, attach piece E to the top of the page, placing it 2" from the left edge, keeping the top edges flush.

2 Attach piece F to the bottom of the page and to the right of piece E, keeping the edges flush.

3 Trim piece G as desired. Attach piece G across the page, on top of piece F, placing it approximately 3/4" from the bottom of the page.

4 Attach the specified photos (photos 2) to the appropriate areas, centering them on the mats.

Tip & Technique
Sewing

Journaling Idea
Title boxes are shown rectangular, but don't be afraid to use a different shape.

For full recipe and Tip & Technique see index pg. 122

© 2005 JRL PUBLICATIONS

ADD AN ELEMENT ADD A SPECIFIC ACCENT TO YOUR LAYOUT FOR CONTINUITY AND FLOW

.... *Cutting Instructions* ....

B&T Paper

A
8 x 8

E
8 x 4

SCRAP

B&T Paper

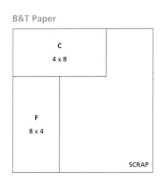

C
4 x 8

F
8 x 4

SCRAP

Cardstock

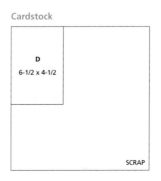

D
6-1/2 x 4-1/2

SCRAP

Cardstock

G 1 x 12

B 1 x 12

SCRAP

© 2005 JRL PUBLICATIONS

KEPT IN PROPORTION KEEP THINGS IN PROPORTION WITH SIMILARLY SIZED ELEMENTS

.... Cutting Instructions ....

B&T Paper

H	A	K
6 x 8	6 x 2	4-1/2 x 3-1/2
SCRAP		

B&T Paper

F	
6 x 10	
L	
6 x 3	SCRAP

B&T Paper

J	B	E
12 x 4	6 x 4	6 x 2
		SCRAP

Cardstock

I	C
4-1/2 x 6-1/2	4-1/2 x 4-1/2
	SCRAP

Cardstock

D	G
4-1/2 x 4-1/2	4-1/2 x 6-1/2
M	
4-1/2 x 5-1/2	SCRAP

© 2005 JRL PUBLICATIONS

Layout Materials

12" x 12" Base Cardstock (2)
12" x 12" Cardstock (2)
12" x 12" B&T Paper (3)

Left Page Dimensions

A 6" x 2"
B 6" x 4"
C 4-1/2" x 4-1/2"
D 4-1/2" x 4-1/2"
E 6" x 2"
F 6" x 10"
G 4-1/2" x 6-1/2"

Right Page Dimensions

H 6" x 8"
I 4-1/2" x 6-1/2"
J 12" x 4"
K 4-1/2" x 3-1/2"
L 6" x 3"
M 4-1/2" x 5-1/2"

Photo Suggestions

1 4" x 4"
2 4" x 6" (2)
3 4" x 5"
4 4" x 3"

Suggested Title/Journaling

1 4" x 4"

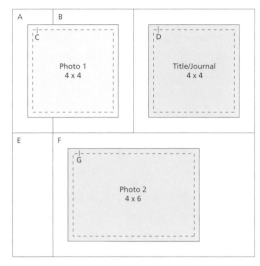

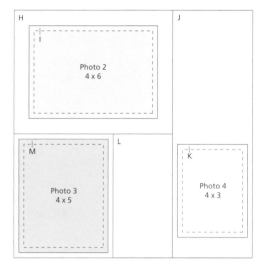

1 Using one 12" x 12" cardstock as your base, attach piece A to the top left corner of the page, keeping the edges flush.

2 Attach piece B to the right of piece A, keeping the edges flush.

3 Attach piece C to the top left corner of the page, placing it 3/4" from the outside edges.

4 Attach piece D to the right of pieces A and B, placing it 3/4" from the left and top edges.

5 Attach piece E to the bottom left corner of the page, keeping side and bottom edges flush.

6 Attach piece F to the bottom right corner of the page, next to piece E, keeping edges flush.

7 Attach piece G to piece F, placing it 3/4" from the bottom and 3/4" from the right edge of piece E.

8 Attach the specified photos (photos 1-2) to the appropriate areas, centering them on the mats.

1 Using one 12" x 12" cardstock as your base, attach piece H to the top left corner of the page, keeping the edges flush.

2 Attach piece I to the center of piece H, placing it 3/4" from all edges.

3 Attach piece J to the right side of the page, keeping the edges flush.

4 Attach piece K to piece J, placing it 1" up from the bottom of the page.

5 Attach piece L to the bottom of the page, keeping the right edge flush with piece J.

6 Attach piece M 1/4" from left and bottom corner of the page.

7 Attach the specified photos (photos 2-4) to the appropriate areas, centering them on the mats.

Kept in Proportion

Tip & Technique
Paper rolling

Journaling Idea
Page titles & journaling can occupy the same space.

For full recipe and Tip & Technique see index pg. 122

© 2005 JRL PUBLICATIONS

Photo Shapes

Layout Materials

12" x 12" Base Cardstock (2)
12" x 12" Cardstock (3)

Left Page Dimensions

A **2" x 4"**
B **6" x 12"**
C **4" x 3"** (2)
D **4" x 3"**

Right Page Dimensions

E **6" x 6"**
F **12" x 6"**
G **6" x 4"**

Photo Suggestions

1 **3" x 3"** (2)
2 **3" circle** (2)
3 **5" x 3-1/2"** (3)
4 **2" x 2"** (3)
5 **3-1/2" x 5"**

Suggested Title

1 **2" x 14"**

Suggested Journaling

1 **3" x 2"**

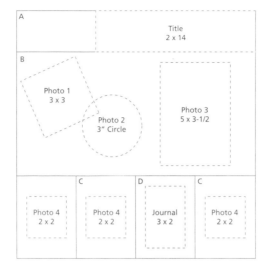

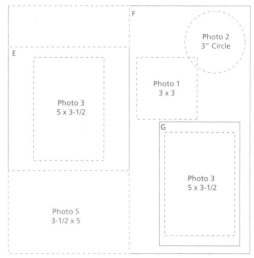

1 Using one 12" x 12" cardstock as your base, attach piece A to the top left corner of the page, keeping the edges flush.

2 Attach piece B across the page, directly below piece A, keeping the side edges flush.

3 Attach one piece C to the bottom right corner of the page, keeping the edges flush.

4 Attach piece D directly to the left of piece C, keeping the edges flush.

5 Attach remaining piece C directly to the left of piece D, keeping the edges flush.

6 Attach the specified photos (photos 1-4) to the appropriate areas, centering them on the mats.

1 Using one 12" x 12" cardstock as your base, attach piece E to the left side of the page 2" down from the top edge, keeping the edges flush.

2 Attach piece F to the right side of the page, keeping the edges flush.

3 Attach piece G to the bottom right corner of piece F, 1/2" from the right and bottom edges of the page.

4 Attach the specified photos (photos 1-3 and 5) to the appropriate areas, centering them on the mats.

Tip & Technique
Making buckles out of paper tags

Journaling Idea
Stamp the background of journaling boxes in various colors.

For full recipe and Tip & Technique see index pg. 122

46

© 2005 JRL PUBLICATIONS

PHOTO SHAPES A VARIETY OF SHAPES COME TOGETHER PERFECTLY

············ *Cutting Instructions* ···

Cardstock

C 4 x 3	C 4 x 3
A 2 x 4	
F 12 x 6	SCRAP

Cardstock

B 6 x 12
E 6 x 6 SCRAP

Cardstock

G 6 x 4
D 4 x 3 SCRAP

© 2005 JRL PUBLICATIONS

all **BOY**

attitude

The Many
faces
Of
Jonathan

It was so fun taking these
pictures of Jonathan for mom.
She loved the result and I
loved the whole process. He
loves to pose with his hand
under his chin it makes me
laugh. Sometimes you pulled
these silly faces and then even
serious ones—just to be funny.
I love you.

dream

WONDER

just goofin' around

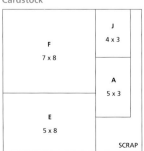
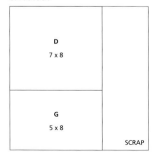
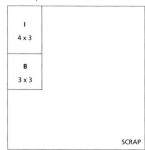
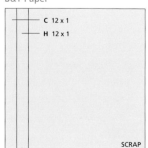

BEAUTY IN REPETITION A COLLECTION OF SMALL PHOTOS CREATES BEAUTY IN REPETITION

·· Cutting Instructions ···········

Cardstock

F 7 x 8	J 4 x 3
	A 5 x 3
E 5 x 8	SCRAP

Cardstock

| D 7 x 8 |
| G 5 x 8 | SCRAP |

B&T Paper

| I 4 x 3 |
| B 3 x 3 |
| SCRAP |

B&T Paper

C 12 x 1
H 12 x 1

SCRAP

© 2005 JRL PUBLICATIONS

Beauty in Repetition

Layout Materials

12" x 12" Base Cardstock (2)
12" x 12" Cardstock (2)
12" x 12" B&T Paper (2)

Left Page Dimensions

A 5" x 3"
B 3" x 3"
C 12" x 1"
D 7" x 8"
E 5" x 8"

Right Page Dimensions

F 7" x 8"
G 5" x 8"
H 12" x 1"
I 4" x 3"
J 4" x 3"

Photo Suggestions

1 3" x 3" (6)
2 4" x 3" (3)
3 6" x 4"

Suggested Title

1 4" x 3"

Suggested Journaling

1 6" x 3"

LEFT

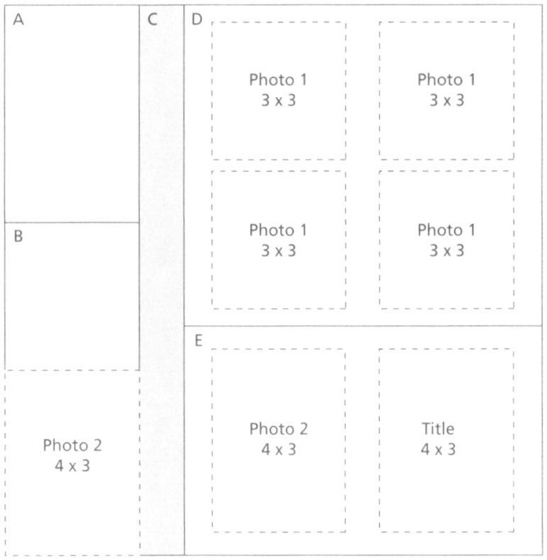
A
C
D
Photo 1 3 x 3
Photo 1 3 x 3
Photo 1 3 x 3
Photo 1 3 x 3
B
E
Photo 2 4 x 3
Photo 2 4 x 3
Title 4 x 3

1 Using one 12" x 12" cardstock as your base, attach piece A to the top left corner of the page, keeping the edges flush.

2 Attach piece B directly under piece A on the left side of the page, keeping the edges flush.

3 Attach piece C down the left side of the page, placing it to the right of pieces A and B, keeping the top and bottom edges flush.

4 Attach piece D to the top right corner of the page, keeping the edges flush.

5 Attach piece E to the bottom right corner of the page, keeping the edges flush.

6 Attach the specified photos (photos 1-2) to the appropriate areas, centering them on the mats.

RIGHT

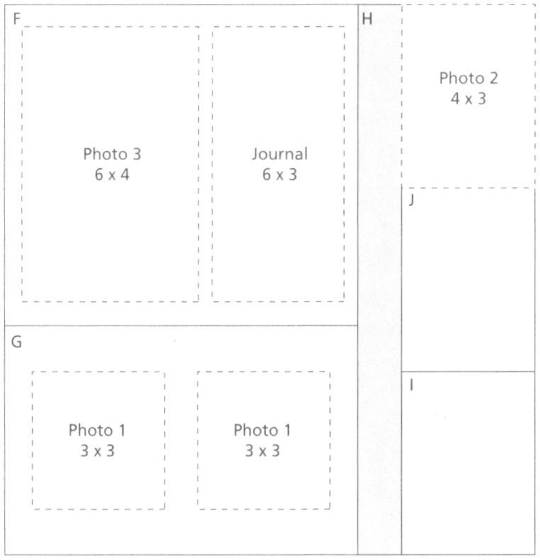
F
H
Photo 2 4 x 3
Photo 3 6 x 4
Journal 6 x 3
J
G
I
Photo 1 3 x 3
Photo 1 3 x 3

1 Using one 12" x 12" cardstock as your base, attach piece F to the top left corner of the page, keeping the edges flush.

2 Attach piece G to the bottom left corner of the page, keeping the edges flush.

3 Attach piece H down the right side of the page, placing it to the right of pieces F and G, keeping the top and bottom edges flush.

4 Attach piece I to the bottom right corner of the page, keeping the edges flush.

5 Attach piece J above piece I, keeping the edges flush.

6 Attach the specified photos (photos 1-3) to the appropriate areas, centering them on the mats.

Tip & Technique

Printing on vellum

Journaling Idea

Add additional titles or journaling to fill empty spaces.

For full recipe and Tip & Technique see index pg. 122

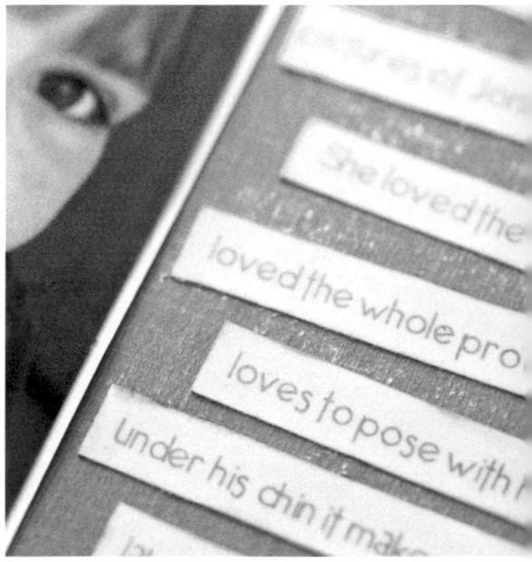
She loved the
loved the whole pro
loves to pose with
Under his chin it

© 2005 JRL PUBLICATIONS

treasure

"GREAT MEMORIES ARE MEANT TO
BE RE-LIVED WITH JOY AND ELATION."

Layout Materials

12" x 12" Base Cardstock (2)
12" x 12" Cardstock (3)
12" x 12" B&T Paper (3)

Left Page Dimensions

A 12" x 6"
B 5" oval
C 4-1/2" x 4-1/2"
D 3" x 6"
E 6" x 6"
F 12" x 1/2"
G 1/2" x 6"
H 1-1/2" circle
I 3" x 3"
J 4-1/2" x 4-1/2"
K 3-3/16" x 3-3/16"

Right Page Dimensions

L 3" x 12"
M 1/2" x 12"
N 6" x 12"
O 4-1/2" x 4-1/2"
P 4-1/2" x 5-1/2"
Q 3" x 3"
R 3" x 3"
S 3" x 3"
T 3" circle
U 1-1/2" circle

Photo Suggestions

1 4-1/2" oval
2 4" x 4" (3)
3 4" x 5" (1)

Suggested Title

1 2" x 8-1/2"

Suggested Journaling

1 2" x 2" (2)

Tip & Technique
Covering buttons

Journaling Idea
Add a title by cutting the paper that is applied to the base page.

For full recipe and Tip & Technique see index pg. 123

LEFT

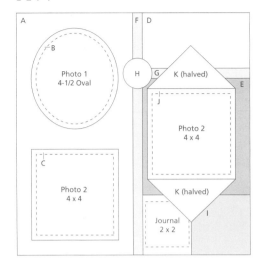

1 Using one 12" x 12" cardstock as your base, attach piece A to the left side of the page, keeping the edges flush.

2 Attach piece B onto the top of piece A, 3/4" from top and left edges.

3 Attach piece C onto the bottom of piece A, 3/4" from bottom and left edges.

4 Attach piece D to top right corner, keeping the top and right edges flush.

5 Attach piece E to the right side of the page below piece D, keeping the edges flush.

6 Attach piece F over the right edge of piece A, overlapping piece D and keeping the edges flush.

7 Attach piece G to the bottom edge of piece D, keeping the right edge flush.

8 Attach one piece H circle over the intersection of pieces F and G.

9 Attach piece I to the bottom right corner of the page, keeping the edges flush.

10 Attach piece J to the center of exposed piece E.

11 Cut piece K in half diagonally. Attach the two pieces to the top and bottom of piece J as shown.

12 Attach the specified photos (photos 1-2) to the appropriate areas, centering them on the mats.

RIGHT

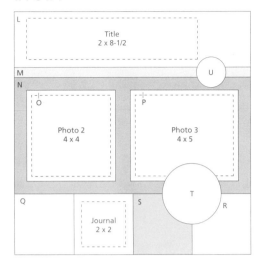

1 Using one 12" x 12" cardstock as your base, attach piece L to the top of the page, keeping the edges flush.

2 Attach piece M to the bottom of piece L, keeping the edges flush.

3 Attach piece N across the center of the page, below pieces L and M, keeping the edges flush.

4 Attach pieces O and P to the center of piece N, placing them approximately 5/8" from the sides and each other.

5 Attach piece Q to the bottom left corner of the page, keeping the edges flush.

6 Attach piece R to the bottom right corner of the page, keeping the edges flush.

7 Attach piece S to the left of piece R, keeping the edges flush.

8 Attach the specified photos (photos 2-3) to the appropriate areas, centering them on the mats.

9 Attach piece T over the intersection of pieces N, R, and S.

10 Attach piece U to piece M, approximately 2" from right edge of the page.

B&T Paper

A 12 x 6	L 3 x 12	R 3 x 3
		H 1-1/2" Circle
		U 1-1/2" Circle
		SCRAP

© 2005 JRL PUBLICATIONS

DREAMY LOOK THIS LAYOUT IS READY TO GO WITH A DREAMY LOOK ALL ITS OWN

········· *Cutting Instructions* ·······································

Cardstock

| T 3" Circle | D 3 x 6 | Q 3 x 3 |
| C 4-1/2 x 4-1/2 | B 5" Oval | |

B&T Paper

| J 4-1/2 x 4-1/2 | O 4-1/2 x 4-1/2 |
| P 4-1/2 x 5-1/2 | K 3-3/16 x 3-3/16 |

SCRAP

B&T Paper

G 1/2 x 6

F 12 x 1/2

M 1/2 x 12

SCRAP

Cardstock

| I 3 x 3 |
| S 3 x 3 |

SCRAP

Cardstock

| N 6 x 12 |
| E 6 x 6 | |

SCRAP

© 2005 JRL PUBLICATIONS

All Because Two People

2004

Fell In Love~

It has always been such a comfort to see how much in love my parents are. After 39 years of marriage, three children, three in-laws and eight grandchildren, they are still going strong. Growing up my mom always told us girls that if we found someone to marry just half the man that our father was that we would be more than lucky. You can see the love that they share for each other by the way that they look at one another and the winks that they share.
-April 2004

The Hansen's

·· *Cutting Instructions* ·············

B&T Paper*

A 9 x 12
SCRAP

B&T Paper*

H 10 x 6	**G** 3 x 6
	SCRAP

Cardstock

F 6 x 8	**B** 3 x 2
J 5 x 5	**J** 5 x 5
	SCRAP

Cardstock

D 2 x 2	**C** 4 x 3
D 2 x 2	
D 2 x 2	**E** 4 x 3
I 2 x 2	
I 2 x 2	
I 2 x 2	SCRAP

*Identical papers

© 2005 JRL PUBLICATIONS

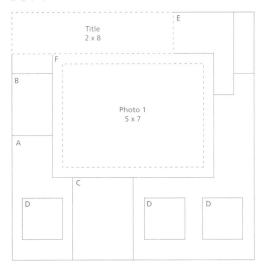

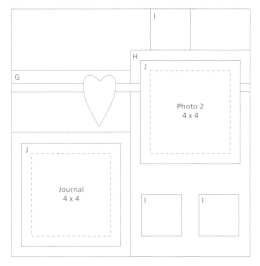

Layout Materials

12" x 12" Base Cardstock (2)
12" x 12" Cardstock (2)
12" x 12" B&T Paper (2)

Left Page Dimensions

A 9" x 12"
B 3" x 2"
C 4" x 3"
D 2" x 2" (3)
E 4" x 3"
F 6" x 8"

Right Page Dimensions

G 3" x 6"
H 10" x 6"
I 2" x 2" (3)
J 5" x 5" (2)

Photo Suggestions

1 5" x 7"
2 4" x 4"

Suggested Title

1 2" x 8"

Suggested Journaling

1 4" x 4"

1 Using one 12" x 12" cardstock as your base, attach piece A to the bottom of the page, keeping the edges flush.

2 Attach piece B to the upper left corner of piece A, keeping the edges flush.

3 Attach piece C to the bottom of the page, placing it 3" from the left edge, keeping the bottom edges flush.

4 Arrange three piece D squares across the bottom of the page, placing them 1" from the bottom and approximately 1/2" from the sides and piece C.

5 Attach piece E to the page, placing it 1" from the left edge and keeping the top edges flush.

6 Attach piece F to the top of the page, placing it next to piece B on top of piece E.

7 Attach the specified photo (photo 1) to the appropriate area, centering it on the mat.

1 Using one 12" x 12" cardstock as your base, attach piece G to the left side of the page, placing it 3" down from the top and keeping the side edges flush.

2 Attach piece H to the bottom right corner of the page, keeping the edges flush.

3 Attach piece I to the top of the page, placing it 3" from the right edge and keeping the top edges flush.

4 Attach the two I pieces to the bottom right, placing them 1" from the bottom, 1/2" from the right, and 1" from each other.

5 Attach one piece J to the bottom left corner of the page, placing it 1/2" from the bottom and 1/2" from the left edges.

6 Attach one piece J to the top of piece H, 2-1/2" down from the top of the page and 1/2" from the edge of the page.

7 Attach the specified photo (photo 2) to the appropriate area, centering it on the mat.

Tip & Technique
Empressor® Guide

Journaling Idea
Adding colored vellum to dark cardstock makes journaling stand out.

For full recipe and Tip & Technique see index pg. 123

© 2005 JRL PUBLICATIONS

Layout Materials

12" x 12" Base Cardstock (2)
12" x 12" Cardstock (1)
12" x 12" B&T Paper (3)

Left Page Dimensions

A 4" x 3"
B 1" x 9"
C 3" circle
D 6" x 12"
E 5" x 5"
F 2" x 12"
G 1" x 3-1/2"

Right Page Dimensions

H 4" x 4"
I 2" x 4"
J 12" x 1"
K 12" x 1"
L 12" x 6"
M 1" x 5-1/2"
N 7" x 5"

Photo Suggestions

1 4" x 4"
2 3" x 3"
3 6" x 4"

Suggested Title

1 4" x 4"

Suggested Journaling

1 3-1/2" x 5-1/2"

LEFT

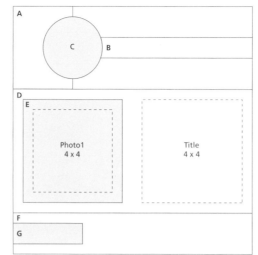

Pieces labeled: A, C (3" circle), B, D, E, Photo1 4 x 4, Title 4 x 4, F, G

RIGHT

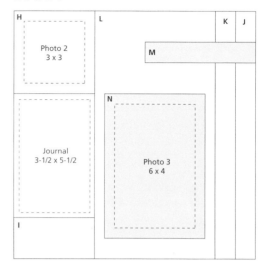

Pieces labeled: H, Photo 2 3 x 3, L, K, J, M, N, Journal 3-1/2 x 5-1/2, Photo 3 6 x 4, I

LEFT

1 Using one 12" x 12" cardstock as your base, attach piece A to the top left corner of the page, keeping the edges flush.

2 Attach piece B to the top right of the page, placing it 1-1/2" down from the top and keeping the side edges flush.

3 Center and attach piece C over the intersection of pieces A and B, placing it 1/2" down from the top edge.

4 Attach piece D across the page below piece A, keeping the side edges flush.

5 Attach piece E to the left side of piece D, placing it 1/2" from the side and top edges.

6 Attach piece F to the bottom of the page, keeping the edges flush.

7 Attach piece G on the left side of piece F, placing it 1/2" from the bottom and keeping the left edges flush.

8 Attach the specified photo (photo 1) to the appropriate area, centering it on the mat.

RIGHT

1 Using one 12" x 12" cardstock as your base, attach piece H to the top left corner of the page, keeping the edges flush.

2 Attach piece I to the bottom left corner of the page, keeping the edges flush.

3 Attach piece J to the right side of the page, keeping the edges flush.

4 Attach piece K to the left of piece J, keeping the edges flush.

5 Attach piece L to the left of piece K, keeping the edges flush.

6 Attach piece M to the right of the page, placing it 1-1/2" from the top and keeping the right edges flush.

7 Attach piece N to the bottom of piece L, placing it 1" from the bottom and 1/2" from the left edge.

8 Attach the specified photos (photos 2-3) to the appropriate areas, centering them on the mats.

Tip & Technique
Printing on My Stickease™ artwork

Journaling Idea
Draw attention to journaling by mixing it with embellishments.

For full recipe and Tip & Technique see index pg. 123

© 2005 JRL PUBLICATIONS

ELEGANT SHOWCASE COMBINE PHOTOS, JOURNALING, AND EMBELLISHMENTS TO SHOWCASE A TREASURED EVENT

Along life's *journey* we are lucky to have a *father* who walks beside us.

Richer than kings I will always be, I had a *father* who spent time with me.

·········· *Cutting Instructions* ··

B&T Paper

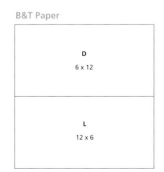

D
6 x 12

L
12 x 6

B&T Paper

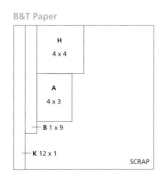

H
4 x 4

A
4 x 3

B 1 x 9

K 12 x 1

SCRAP

B&T Paper

I
2 x 4

F
2 x 12

J 12 x 1

SCRAP

Cardstock

M 1 x 5-1/2

G 1 x 3-1/2

N
7 x 5

C
3 " circle

E
5 x 5

SCRAP

© 2005 JRL PUBLICATIONS

Makenna and Julia

A NEW PERSPECTIVE YOUR ARTWORK WILL FLOW BEAUTIFULLY WITH THIS NEW PERSPECTIVE

Cutting Instructions

B&T Paper*

A
11 x 11

SCRAP

B&T Paper*

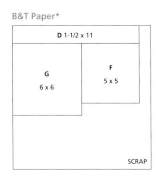

D 1-1/2 x 11

G
6 x 6

F
5 x 5

SCRAP

Cardstock**

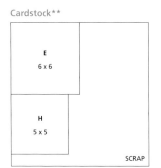

E
6 x 6

H
5 x 5

SCRAP

Cardstock**

B
10 x 10

SCRAP

B&T Paper

C
8 x 8

SCRAP

*Identical papers   **Identical papers

© 2005 JRL PUBLICATIONS

© 2005 JRL PUBLICATIONS

Layout Materials

12" x 12" Base Cardstock (2)
12" x 12" Cardstock (2)
12" x 12" B&T Paper (3)

Left Page Dimensions

A 11" x 11"
B 10" x 10"
C 8" x 8"
D 1-1/2" x 11"

Right Page Dimensions

E 6" x 6"
F 5" x 5"
G 6" x 6"
H 5" x 5"

Photo Suggestions

1 5" x 7"
2 4" x 4"
3 3" x 3" (8)

Suggested Title

1 1" x 10"

Suggested Journaling

1 4" x 4"

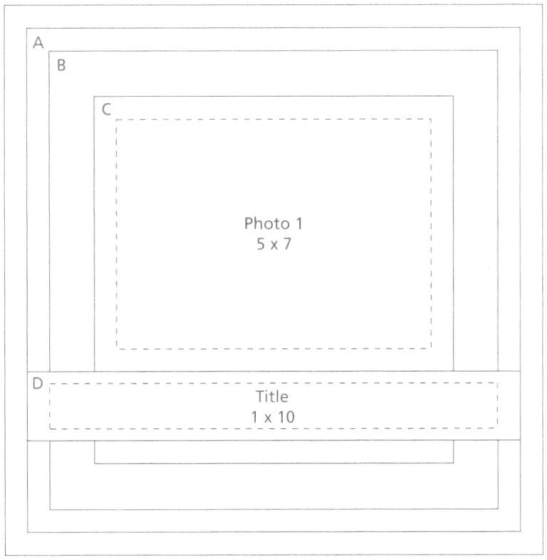

A
B
C

Photo 1
5 x 7

D
Title
1 x 10

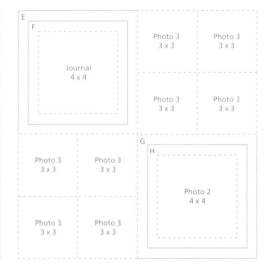

E
F

Journal
4 x 4

Photo 3
3 x 3

Photo 3
3 x 3

Photo 3
3 x 3

Photo 3
3 x 3

Photo 3
3 x 3

Photo 3
3 x 3

G
H

Photo 2
4 x 4

Photo 3
3 x 3

Photo 3
3 x 3

Left

1 Using one 12" x 12" cardstock as your base, attach piece A to the center of the page, keeping 1/2" on all sides.

2 Attach piece B to the top of piece A, centered with 1/2" on all sides.

3 Attach piece C to the top of piece B, centered with 1" on all sides.

4 Attach piece D on top of pieces A, B, and C, 2-1/2" from the bottom of the page.

5 Attach the specified photo (photo 1) to the appropriate area, centering it on the mat.

Right

1 Using one 12" x 12" cardstock as your base, attach piece E to the top left corner of the page, keeping the edges flush.

2 Attach piece F to the top of piece E, keeping 1/2" from the edge of piece E.

3 Attach piece G to the bottom right corner of the page, keeping the edges flush.

4 Attach piece H to the top of piece G, keeping 1/2" from the edge of piece G.

5 Attach the specified photos (photos 2-3) to the appropriate areas, centering them on the mats.

A New Perspective

Tip & Technique
Dividing photo designations

Journaling Idea
Use metal embellishments to creatively attach titles or journaling to your page.

For full recipe and Tip & Technique see index pg. 123

Layout Materials

12" x 12" Base Cardstock (2)
12" x 12" Cardstock (3)
12" x 12" B&T Paper (1)

Left Page Dimensions

A 2" x 12"
B 3" circle
C 7" x 12"
D 3" x 3" (4)

Right Page Dimensions

E 12" x 7"
F 12" x 6"
G 7" x 5"

Photo Suggestions

1 3" x 3" (4)
2 6" x 4"

Suggested Title

1 1-1/2" x 6-1/2"

Suggested Journaling

1 3" x 3" (3)

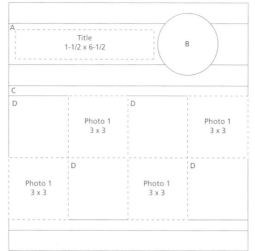

A — Title 1-1/2 x 6-1/2
B
C
D — Photo 1 3 x 3 — Photo 1 3 x 3
D — Photo 1 3 x 3 — Photo 1 3 x 3

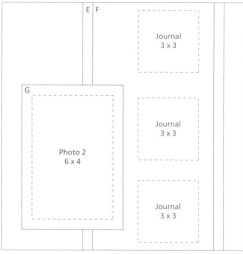

E F
Journal 3 x 3
G
Photo 2 6 x 4
Journal 3 x 3
Journal 3 x 3

1 Using one 12" x 12" cardstock as your base, attach piece A across the top of the page, placing it 1" from the top, keeping the edges flush.

2 Attach piece B to the right side of piece A, placing it 1/2" from the top and 1-1/2" from the right edge.

3 Attach piece C across the bottom of the page, placing it 1" from the bottom edge, keeping the side edges flush.

4 Arrange four piece D squares on piece C in the specified checkerboard pattern; attach.

5 Arrange four photos (photos 1) in the alternating diagonal spots across piece C.

1 Using one 12" x 12" cardstock as your base, attach piece E down the right side of the page, placing it 1" from the right edge, keeping the top and bottom edges flush.

2 Attach piece F to the center of piece E, placing it 1/2" from the edge, keeping the top and bottom edges flush.

3 Attach piece G to the left side of the page, placing it 1" from the bottom and left edges.

4 Attach the specified photo (photo 2) to the appropriate area, centering it on the mat.

Tip & Technique
Direct-to-paper ink

Journaling Idea
Use multiple journaling boxes to convey a variety of thoughts.

For full recipe and Tip & Technique see index pg. 123

© 2005 JRL PUBLICATIONS

.... *Cutting Instructions* ....

Cardstock*

C 7 x 12	
A 2 x 12	
	SCRAP

Cardstock*

E 12 x 7	
	SCRAP

B&T Paper

F 12 x 6	**D** 3 x 3
	D 3 x 3
	D 3 x 3
	D 3 x 3
	SCRAP

Cardstock

G 7 x 5	
B 3" Circle	
	SCRAP

© 2005 JRL PUBLICATIONS

*Identical papers

Cooking WITH Mom

How to Bake Cookies
(When you're the Mom)

·· *Cutting Instructions* ···········

Cardstock

E 4 x 12	**A** 10 x 8
	SCRAP

B&T Paper

C 12 x 2
SCRAP

Cardstock

G 2 x 10
D 1 x 6
H 1 x 6
SCRAP

Cardstock

F 12 x 6	**B** 2 x 8
	SCRAP

© 2005 JRL PUBLICATIONS

Layout Materials

12" x 12" Base Cardstock (2)
12" x 12" Cardstock (3)
12" x 12" B&T Paper (1)

Left Page Dimensions

A 10" x 8"
B 2" x 8"
C 12" x 2"
D 1" x 6"

Right Page Dimensions

E 4" x 12"
F 12" x 6"
G 2" x 10"
H 1" x 6"

Photo Suggestions

1 8" x 6"
2 2" x 2" (4)
3 3" x 3" (2)

Suggested Title

1 1-1/2" x 8"

Suggested Journaling

1 6" x 4"

LEFT

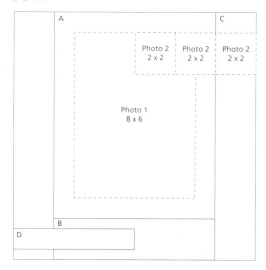

A

Photo 2
2 x 2   Photo 2
2 x 2   Photo 2
2 x 2

Photo 1
8 x 6

B

C

D

RIGHT

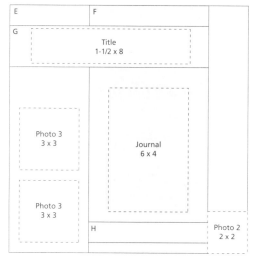

E   F

G

Title
1-1/2 x 8

Photo 3
3 x 3

Journal
6 x 4

Photo 3
3 x 3

H   Photo 2
2 x 2

1 Using one 12" x 12" cardstock as your base, attach piece A to the top of the page, 2" from the left edge, keeping the top edges flush.

2 Attach piece B to the bottom of the page, 2" from the left edge and directly under piece A, keeping the edges flush.

3 Attach piece C to the right of the page, flush with pieces A and B, keeping the edges flush.

4 Attach piece D to the bottom left corner of the page, 1/2" from the bottom, keeping the edges flush.

5 Attach the specified photos (photos 1-2) to the appropriate areas, centering them on the mats and as shown.

1 Using one 12" x 12" cardstock as your base, attach piece E to the left of the page, keeping the edges flush.

2 Attach piece F directly next to piece E, keeping the edges flush.

3 Attach piece G across the page, on top of pieces E and F, 1" from the top of the page, keeping left edges flush.

4 Attach piece H on top of piece F, 1" from the bottom edge, keeping the side edges flush.

5 Attach the specified photos (photos 2-3) to the appropriate areas, centering them on the mats.

Tip & Technique

Using photos as B&T paper

Journaling Idea

If you would like to add a mat to a photo or journaling box, simply add ½" to both the height and width.

For full recipe and Tip & Technique see index pg. 124

© 2005 JRL PUBLICATIONS

Layout Materials

12" x 12" Base Cardstock (2)
12" x 12" Cardstock (3)
12" x 12" B&T Paper (1)

Left Page Dimensions

A 4" x 12"
B 4" x 6"
C 2" x 2" (5)
D 4" x 4"
E 4" x 4"
F 1/2" x 12"

Right Page Dimensions

G 8" x 6"
H 7" x 5"
I 6" x 4"
J 4" x 6" (2)
K 4" x 6"
L 2" x 2" (3)
M 1/2" x 12"

Photo Suggestions

1 4" x 3" (3)
2 4" x 4"
3 4" x 6"
4 3" x 5" (2)

Suggested Title

1 3-1/2" x 11"

Suggested Journaling

1 3" x 3"

LEFT

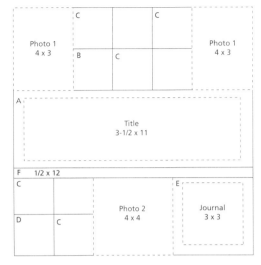

RIGHT

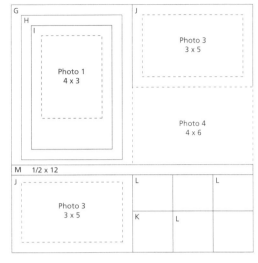

LEFT

1 Using one 12" x 12" cardstock as your base, attach piece A across the center of the page 4" down from the top of the page, keeping the side edges flush.

2 Prepare piece B by attaching pieces C in a checkerboard pattern as shown.

3 Attach piece B to the top center of the page, 3" from the left and right edges of the page, keeping the top edges flush.

4 Attach two piece C squares to the opposite corners of piece D, keeping the edges flush.

5 Attach piece D to the bottom left corner of the page, keeping the edges flush.

6 Attach piece E to the bottom right corner of the page, keeping the edges flush.

7 Attach the specified photos (photos 1-2) to the appropriate areas, keeping the edges flush.

8 Attach piece F on top of pieces A, C, D, and E.

RIGHT

1 Using one 12" x 12" cardstock as your base, attach piece G to the top left corner of the page, keeping the edges flush.

2 Center piece H mat to the top of piece G.

3 Center piece I mat to the top of piece H.

4 Attach one piece J to the top right corner of the page, keeping the edges flush.

5 Attach remaining piece J to the bottom left corner of the page, keeping the edges flush.

6 Prepare piece K by attaching pieces L in a checkerboard pattern as shown.

7 Attach piece K to the bottom right corner of the page, keeping the edges flush.

8 Attach the specified photos (photos 1, 3, and 4) to the appropriate areas, centering them on the existing mats.

9 Attach piece M on top of piece G, J, K, and L.

Tip & Technique

Make empty spots pop

Journaling Idea

Create a border for your title with repeating words or phrases.

For full recipe and Tip & Technique see index pg. 124

© 2005 JRL PUBLICATIONS

Cutting Instructions

Cardstock

A
4 x 12

G
8 x 6

B&T Paper

J		J	
4 x 6		4 x 6	

E	C	C	C	L
	2 x 2	2 x 2	2 x 2	2 x 2
4 x 4	C	C	L	L
	2 x 2	2 x 2	2 x 2	2 x 2

SCRAP

Cardstock

B	K
4 x 6	4 x 6

H	D
7 x 5	4 x 4

SCRAP

Cardstock

	F 1/2 x 12	M 1/2 x 12
I		
6 x 4		

SCRAP

© 2005 JRL PUBLICATIONS

ABSTRACT THIS ABSTRACT DESIGN BOASTS APPEAL WITH A PERFECT BALANCE

.... Cutting Instructions ....

B&T Paper

M 6 x 6
A 12 x 6
G 3 x 6
SCRAP

B&T Paper

E 4 x 6
H 9 x 6
SCRAP

Cardstock

	D 2-3/4 x 5
F 7 x 5	I 1/2 x 6
	C 1/2 x 6
	J 1-1/2 x 2-1/2
L 5 x 5	SCRAP

Cardstock

B 7 x 5	K 7 x 5
	SCRAP

© 2005 JRL PUBLICATIONS

Layout Materials

12" x 12" Base Cardstock (2)
12" x 12" Cardstock (2)
12" x 12" B&T Paper (2)

Left Page
Dimensions

A   12" x 6"
B   7" x 5"
C   1/2" x 6"
D   2-3/4" x 5"
E   4" x 6"
F   7" x 5"

Right Page
Dimensions

G   3" x 6"
H   9" x 6"
I   1/2" x 6"
J   1-1/2" x 2-1/2"
K   7" x 5"
L   5" x 5"
M   6" x 6"

Photo
Suggestions

1   6" x 4" (3)
2   4-1/2" circle

Suggested Title

1   2-1/2" x 4-3/4"

Suggested
Journaling

1   3" x 3" (2)

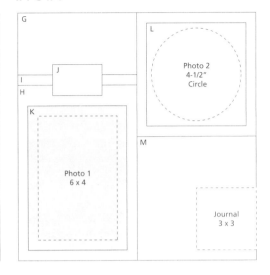

Diagram labels — Left page: A, B, E, Journal 3 x 3, Photo 1 6 x 4, F, D, Photo 1 6 x 4, C, Title 2-1/2 x 4-3/4. Right page: G, L, J, I, H, Photo 2 4-1/2" Circle, K, M, Photo 1 6 x 4, Journal 3 x 3.

1 Using one 12" x 12" cardstock as your base, attach piece A to the left of the page, keeping the edges flush.

2 Attach piece B onto piece A, placing it 1/2" from the top and left edges.

3 Attach piece C onto piece A, placing it 2" from the bottom, keeping the side edges flush.

4 Attach piece D over piece C, placing it 1" from the bottom and 1/2" from the left edge.

5 Attach piece E to the top right corner of the page, keeping the edges flush.

6 Attach piece F to the bottom right of the page, placing it 1/2" from the right and bottom edges.

7 Attach the specified photos (photo 1) to the appropriate areas, centering them on the mats.

1 Using one 12" x 12" cardstock as your base, attach piece G to the top left corner of the page, keeping the edges flush.

2 Attach piece H to the bottom left corner of the page, keeping the edges flush.

3 Attach piece I centered over the edges of pieces G and H, keeping the side edges flush.

4 Center and attach piece J onto piece I.

5 Attach piece K onto piece H, placing it 1/2" from the left and 1/2" from the bottom edge.

6 Attach piece L to the top right of the page, placing it 1/2" from the top and right edges.

7 Attach piece M to the bottom right corner of the page, keeping the edges flush.

8 Attach the specified photos (photos 1-2) to the appropriate areas, centering them on the mats.

Abstract

Tip & Technique
Fill with embellishments

Journaling Idea
Hidden journaling keeps personal messages private.

For full recipe and Tip & Technique see index pg. 124

© 2005 JRL PUBLICATIONS

Layout Materials

12" x 12" Base Cardstock (2)
12" x 12" Cardstock (4)

Left Page Dimensions

A 10" x 10"
B 9" x 9"

Right Page Dimensions

C 6" x 6"
D 5" x 5"
E 6" x 6"
F 3" x 3"

Photo Suggestions

1 8" x 8"
2 4" x 4" (2)
3 3" x 3" (3)

Suggested Title

1 1-1/2" x 6"

Suggested Journaling

1 1-1/2" x 6"

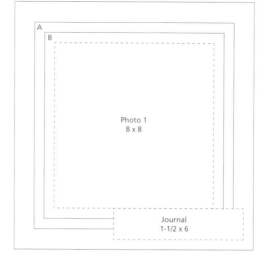

A

B

Photo 1
8 x 8

Journal
1-1/2 x 6

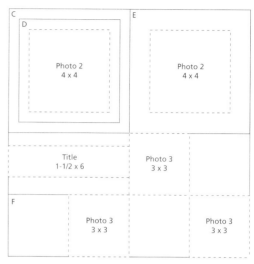

C
D

Photo 2
4 x 4

E

Photo 2
4 x 4

Title
1-1/2 x 6

Photo 3
3 x 3

F

Photo 3
3 x 3

Photo 3
3 x 3

1 Using one 12" x 12" cardstock as your base, attach piece A to the center of the page, leaving a 1" border on all sides.

2 Attach piece B to the center of piece A, leaving a 1/2" border on all sides.

3 Attach the specified photo (photo 1) to the appropriate area, centering it on the mat.

1 Using one 12" x 12" cardstock as your base, attach piece C to the top left corner of the page, keeping the edges flush.

2 Attach piece D to the center of piece C, leaving a 1/2" border on all sides.

3 Attach piece E to the top right corner of the page, keeping the edges flush.

4 Attach piece F to the bottom left corner of the page, keeping the edges flush.

5 Attach specified photos (photos 2-3) to the appropriate areas, centering them on the mats.

Tip & Technique
Accenting
with ribbon

Journaling Idea
Draw attention
to journaling
by placing it on
the diagonal.

For full recipe and Tip & Technique see index pg. 124

© 2005 JRL PUBLICATIONS

Our family had so much fun this year at Disneyland. We had the best of both worlds this year. Mom enjoyed the princesses with Kaitlyn and Dad got a kick out of the action heros. Our one regret: missing Bob Incredible by just one week.

What a bunch of characters!

UNIFIED WHOLE COMBINE MANY SMALL PIECES TO COMPOSE A UNIFIED WHOLE

············· *Cutting Instructions* ·······························

Cardstock*

> B
> 9 x 9
>
> SCRAP

Cardstock*

> C
> 6 x 6
>
> SCRAP

Cardstock**

> E
> 6 x 6
>
> F
> 3 x 3
>
> D
> 5 x 5
>
> SCRAP

Cardstock**

> A
> 10 x 10
>
> SCRAP

© 2005 JRL PUBLICATIONS

*Identical papers **Identical papers

Hawaii

Our trip to Oahu, Hawaii

February 23- March 2, 2006

We rented scooters and cruised around the island.

We had so much fun!

beach

PARADISE

D E S I G N E R ' S   E Y E   HAVE SOME FUN WITH THIS LAYOUT PUT TOGETHER WITH A DESIGNER'S EYE

··· Cutting Instructions ··············

Cardstock

C 7 x 6	**J** 7 x 6	
E 4 x 2-1/2	**K** — 2-1/2 x 2-1/2	SCRAP

B&T Paper

F 7 x 6	
A 4-1/2 x 6	SCRAP

B&T Paper

B 4-1/2 x 3	
G 4-1/2 x 3	
H 3 x 3	SCRAP

B&T Paper

D 1 x 12
I 2 x 6
SCRAP

© 2005 JRL PUBLICATIONS

Layout Materials

12" x 12" Base Cardstock (2)
12" x 12" Cardstock (1)
12" x 12" B&T Paper (3)

Left Page Dimensions

A 4-1/2" x 6"
B 4-1/2" x 3"
C 7" x 6"
D 1" x 12"
E 4" x 2-1/2"

Right Page Dimensions

F 7" x 6"
G 4-1/2" x 3"
H 3" x 3"
I 2" x 6"
J 7" x 6"
K 2-1/2" x 2-1/2"

Photo Suggestions

1 3-1/2" x 5" (2)
2 6" x 4" (3)

Suggested Title

1 2" x 12"

Suggested Journaling

1 2" x 6"

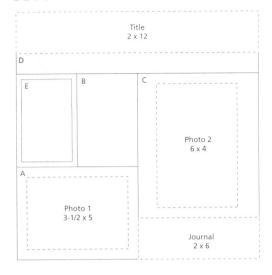

Left page layout diagram:
- Title 2 x 12
- D
- E — 4" x 2-1/2"
- B
- C
- A
- Photo 2 6 x 4
- Photo 1 3-1/2 x 5
- Journal 2 x 6

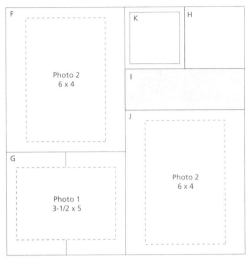

Right page layout diagram:
- F
- K
- H
- Photo 2 6 x 4
- I
- J
- G
- Photo 1 3-1/2 x 5
- Photo 2 6 x 4

LEFT

1 Using one 12" x 12" cardstock as your base, attach piece A to the bottom left corner of the page, keeping the edges flush.

2 Attach piece B directly above piece A, placing it 3" from the left edge.

3 Attach piece C to the right side of the page, placing it 2" up from the bottom edge, keeping the side edges flush.

4 Attach piece D directly above pieces B and C, keeping the edges flush.

5 Attach piece E 1/4" from the edge of the page and 1/4" below piece D.

6 Attach the specified photos (photos 1-2) to the appropriate areas, centering them on the mats.

RIGHT

1 Using one 12" x 12" cardstock as your base, attach piece F to the top left corner of the page, keeping the edges flush.

2 Attach piece G to the bottom left corner of the page, keeping edges flush.

3 Attach piece H to the top right corner of the page, keeping the edges flush.

4 Attach piece I below piece H, keeping the edges flush.

5 Attach piece J to the bottom right corner of the page, keeping the edges flush.

6 Attach piece K 1/4" from top edge of the page, centered between pieces F and H.

7 Attach the specified photos (photos 1-2) to the appropriate areas, centering them on the mats.

Designer's Eye

Tip & Technique
Watercolor

Journaling Idea
Don't be afraid to place the title and journaling on the same page.

For full recipe and Tip & Technique see index pg. 124

© 2005 JRL PUBLICATIONS

Layout Materials

12" x 12" Base Cardstock (2)
12" x 12" Cardstock (1)
12" x 12" B&T Paper (2)

Left Page Dimensions

A **12" x 1-1/2"**
B **12" x 4-1/2"**
C **6" x 6"**
D **1-1/2" x 6"**

Right Page Dimensions

E **6" x 6"**
F **6" x 6"**
G **1-1/2" x 12"**
H **3-1/2" x 12"**

Photo Suggestions

1 **6" x 4"**
2 **4" x 4"** (3)
3 **4" x 6"**

Suggested Title

1 **1-1/2" x 6"**

Suggested Journaling

1 **3-1/2" x 2-1/2"**

LEFT

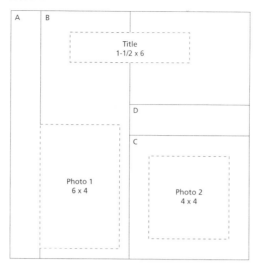

A | B
Title
1-1/2 x 6
D
C
Photo 1
6 x 4
Photo 2
4 x 4

RIGHT

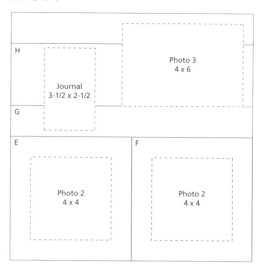

H
Photo 3
4 x 6
Journal
3-1/2 x 2-1/2
G
E | F
Photo 2
4 x 4
Photo 2
4 x 4

1 Using one 12" x 12" cardstock as your base, attach piece A to the left side of the page, keeping the edges flush.

2 Attach piece B to the page, placing it to the right of piece A, keeping the edges flush.

3 Attach piece C to the bottom right corner of the page, keeping the edges flush.

4 Attach piece D directly above piece C, keeping the edges flush.

5 Attach the specified photos (photos 1-2) to the appropriate areas, centering them on the mats.

1 Using one 12" x 12" cardstock as your base, attach piece E to the bottom left corner of the page, keeping the edges flush.

2 Attach piece F to the bottom right corner of the page, keeping the edges flush.

3 Attach piece G directly above pieces E and F, keeping the edges flush.

4 Attach piece H directly above piece G, keeping the edges flush.

5 Attach the specified photos (photos 2-3) to the appropriate areas, centering them on the mats.

Tip & Technique
Softening edges

Journaling Idea
Find a quote from someone you admire to adequately express feelings and sentiments.

For full recipe and Tip & Technique see index pg. 125

© 2005 JRL PUBLICATIONS

MEMORIES

Two people
growing so close
they discover
Their happiness
always is found
in each other.
Two people
seeing loves
sweet dream come
true...
This is the
meaning of
marriage.

FAMILY

Beautiful
Bride

Cutting
the Cake

Eating
the Cake

SIMPLE PLEASURES IT'S SIMPLY PLEASURABLE TO CREATE PAGES AS BEAUTIFUL AS THESE

·········· *Cutting Instructions* ··········

B&T Paper

A 12 x 1-1/2

G 1-1/2 x 12

D 1-1/2 x 6

SCRAP

Cardstock

E	C
6 x 6	6 x 6

H
4-1/2 x 12

SCRAP

B&T Paper

F
6 x 6

B
12 x 4-1/2

SCRAP

© 2005 JRL PUBLICATIONS

FAB FIFTEEN BELIEVE IT OR NOT, FIFTEEN PHOTOS FIT ONTO THIS FABULOUS LAYOUT

·· *Cutting Instructions* ·············

B&T Paper

| **C** 1/2 x 12 |
| **G** 1/2 x 12 |
| **G** 1/2 x 12 |

SCRAP

B&T Paper

| **B** |
| 2 x 4 |
| **B** |
| 2 x 4 |
| **D** |
| 2 x 4 |

SCRAP

Cardstock

| **A** 4 x 8 | **E** 4 x 4 |
| **F** 2 x 2 / **F** 2 x 2 | |

SCRAP

© 2005 JRL PUBLICATIONS

Layout Materials

12" x 12" Base Cardstock (2)
12" x 12" Cardstock (1)
12" x 12" B&T Paper (2)

Left Page Dimensions

A 4" x 8"
B 2" x 4" (2)
C 1/2" x 12"

Right Page Dimensions

D 2" x 4"
E 4" x 4"
F 2" x 2" (2)
G 1/2" x 12" (2)

Photo Suggestions

1 6" x 4" (3)
2 4" x 4" (7)
3 2" x 2" (4)
4 3" x 3"

Suggested Title/Journaling

1 3" x 7"

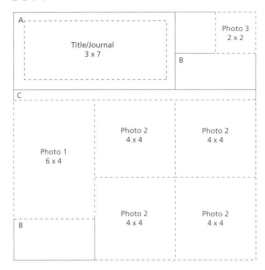

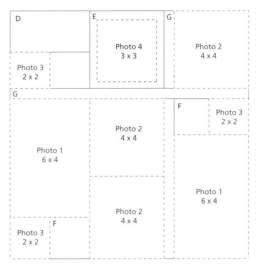

1 Using one 12" x 12" cardstock as your base, attach piece A to the top left of the page, keeping the edges flush.

2 Attach one piece B to the right edge of piece A, 2" from the top, keeping the right edges flush with the page.

3 Attach remaining piece B to the bottom left edge of the page, keeping the side edges flush.

4 Arrange the specified photos (photos 1-3), carefully keeping the edges flush against each other, and attach.

5 Attach piece C to the bottom edge of pieces A and B, keeping the side edges flush.

1 Using one 12" x 12" cardstock as your base, attach piece D to the top left corner of the page, keeping the edges flush.

2 Attach piece E to the page to the right of piece D, keeping the edges of the page flush.

3 Attach one piece F to the right side of the page, 2" from the edge and 4" from the top of the page.

4 Attach remaining piece F to the bottom left corner 2" from the left edge of the page, keeping the bottom edges flush.

5 Arrange the specified photos (photos 1-4) to the appropriate areas of the page, carefully keeping the edges flush against each other, and attach.

6 Attach one piece G strip to the page vertically between pieces E and F.

7 Attach remaining piece G strip next to piece C on left side of the page, keeping left and right edges flush.

Tip & Technique
Stamping on ribbon

Journaling Idea
Carry ideas across both pages by adding a simple vellum tag.

For full recipe and Tip & Technique see index pg. 125

75

© 2005 JRL PUBLICATIONS

Layout Materials

12" x 12" Base Cardstock (2)
12" x 12" Cardstock (1)
12" x 12" B&T Paper (3)

Left Page Dimensions

A **12" x 8"**
B **12" x 4"**
C **6" x 12"**

Right Page Dimensions

D **12" x 8"**
E **12" x 4"**
F **6" x 12"**

Photo Suggestions

1 **4" x 6"**
2 **3" x 3"**
3 **5" x 3-1/2"** (2)

Suggested Title

1 **4" x 5"**

Suggested Journaling

1 **5" x 3-1/2"**

LEFT

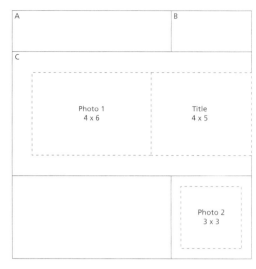

RIGHT

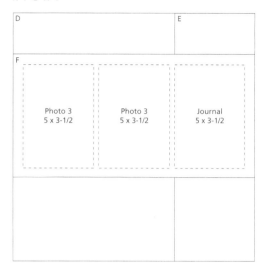

1 Using one 12" x 12" cardstock as your base, attach piece A to the left side of the page, keeping the edges flush.

2 Attach piece B to the right side of the page, keeping the edges flush.

3 Attach piece C across the page, placing it 2" down from the top and keeping the side edges flush.

4 Attach the specified photos (photos 1-2) to the appropriate areas.

1 Using one 12" x 12" cardstock as your base, attach piece D to the left side of the page, keeping the edges flush.

2 Attach piece E to the right side of the page, keeping the edges flush.

3 Attach piece F across pieces D and E, placing it 2" from the top and keeping the edges flush.

4 Attach the specified photos (photos 3) to the appropriate areas.

Tip & Technique
Foil

Journaling Idea
Connect your title and photo using vellum and a large monogram.

For full recipe and Tip & Technique see index pg. 125

© 2005 JRL PUBLICATIONS

summer TIME
fun

July 2005
Jackson & Kate

summer is our favorite holiday at our house

because we can spend all day out

in the hot Utah sun and besides, what

is better on a hot day than the Slip n Slide?

Jackson and Kate had such a blast

spending the day splashing in the water!

The one day that I didn't want

to get wet, they soaked me while I was taking pictures!

PORTRAIT COLLECTION **THIS DESIGN IS IDEAL FOR CONTRASTING A COLLECTION OF PORTRAITS**

.... *Cutting Instructions* ....

Cardstock

D 12 x 8	B 12 x 4

B&T Paper

C 6 x 12	E 12 x 4
	SCRAP

B&T Paper*

F 6 x 12
SCRAP

B&T Paper*

A 12 x 8	
	SCRAP

© 2005 JRL PUBLICATIONS

*Identical papers

ACCENT EMPHASIS   THIS LAYOUT PROVIDES THE PERFECT SHOWCASE FOR SMALL ACCENTS

.... *Cutting Instructions* ....

Cardstock

A
2 x 12

G
2 x 6

C
6-1/2 x 4-1/2

K
4-1/2 x 4-1/2

M
3" Circle

SCRAP

Cardstock

D
8 x 3

L
6 x 3

F
2 x 3

SCRAP

B&T Paper

E
8 x 3

J
6 x 6

SCRAP

B&T Paper

B
8 x 6

I
6 x 3

H
2 x 3

SCRAP

© 2005 JRL PUBLICATIONS

Layout Materials

12" x 12" Base Cardstock (2)
12" x 12" Cardstock (2)
12" x 12" B&T Paper (2)

Left Page Dimensions

A 2" x 12"
B 8" x 6"
C 6-1/2" x 4-1/2"
D 8" x 3"
E 8" x 3"

Right Page Dimensions

F 2" x 3"
G 2" x 6"
H 2" x 3"
I 6" x 3"
J 6" x 6"
K 4-1/2" x 4-1/2"
L 6" x 3"
M 3" circle

Photo Suggestions

1 6" x 4"
2 2" x 2" (5)
3 4" x 4"

Suggested Title

1 2" x 11"

Suggested Journaling

1 5" x 2"

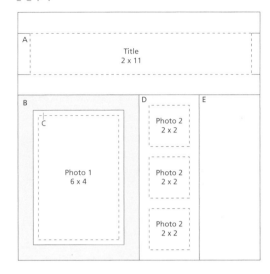

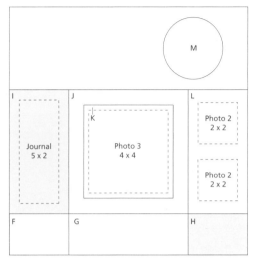

LEFT

1 Using one 12" x 12" cardstock as your base, attach piece A to the top of the page, placing it 1" from the top, keeping the side edges flush.

2 Attach piece B to the bottom left corner of the page, keeping the edges flush.

3 Attach piece C to the center of piece B.

4 Attach piece D to the right of piece B, keeping the side and bottom edges flush.

5 Attach piece E to the bottom right corner of the page, keeping the edges flush.

6 Attach the specified photos (photos 1-2) to the appropriate areas, centering them on the mats.

RIGHT

1 Using one 12" x 12" cardstock as your base, attach piece F to the bottom left corner of the page, keeping the edges flush.

2 Attach piece G to the right of piece F, keeping the side and bottom edges flush.

3 Attach piece H to the bottom right corner of the page, keeping the edges flush.

4 Attach piece I to the left side of the page, directly above piece F, keeping the edges flush.

5 Attach piece J to the right side of piece I directly above piece G.

6 Attach piece K to the center of piece J.

7 Attach piece L to the right side of the page directly above piece H, keeping the edges flush.

8 Attach piece M to the top right of the page, placing it 1/2" from the top and 1-1/2" from the right edges.

9 Attach the specified photos (photos 2-3) to the appropriate areas, centering them on the mats.

Tip & Technique
My Reflections Collection™ kits

Journaling Idea
Accentuate photo details by connecting them to journaling with a fiber and brads.

For full recipe and Tip & Technique see index pg. 125

© 2005 JRL PUBLICATIONS

Layout Materials

12" x 12" Base Cardstock (2)
12" x 12" Cardstock (2)
12" x 12" B&T Paper (1)

Left Page Dimensions

A 3" x 4"
B 6" x 12"
C 4" x 6"
D 3" x 9"
E 3" x 3"
F 2" circle (3)

Right Page Dimensions

G 4" x 6" (2)
H 4" x 6"
I 1" x 12"
J 2" circle (4)

Photo Suggestions

1 3-1/2" x 5-1/2" (4)
2 2-1/2" x 3-1/2" (2)

Suggested Title

1 2-1/2" x 7-1/2"

Suggested Journaling

1 3-1/2" x 5-1/2"

LEFT

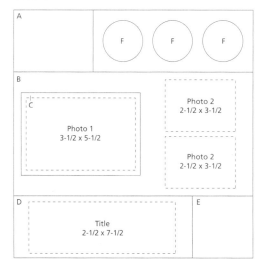

A

B

C

Photo 1
3-1/2 x 5-1/2

Photo 2
2-1/2 x 3-1/2

Photo 2
2-1/2 x 3-1/2

F F F

D

Title
2-1/2 x 7-1/2

E

RIGHT

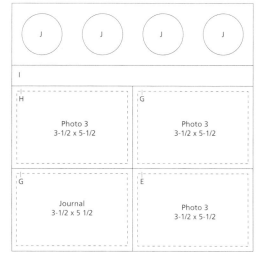

J J J J

I

H

Photo 3
3-1/2 x 5-1/2

G

Photo 3
3-1/2 x 5-1/2

G

Journal
3-1/2 x 5 1/2

E

Photo 3
3-1/2 x 5-1/2

1 Using one 12" x 12" cardstock as your base, attach piece A to the top left corner of the page, keeping edges flush.

2 Attach piece B below piece A, keeping the edges flush.

3 Attach piece C onto piece B, 1/2" from the right edge and 1" below piece A.

4 Attach piece D to the bottom left corner of the page, keeping the edges flush.

5 Attach piece E to the bottom right corner of the page, keeping edges flush.

6 Attach three pieces F to the cardstock at the top of the page, as shown. (We used circles from various colored papers for added interest.)

7 Attach the specified photos (photos 1-2) to the appropriate areas, centering them on the mats.

1 Using one 12" x 12" cardstock as your base, attach one piece G to the bottom left corner of the page, keeping the edges flush.

2 Attach piece H above piece G, keeping the edges flush.

3 Attach remaining piece G to the right of piece H, keeping the side edges flush.

4 Attach piece I above pieces G and H, keeping the side edges flush.

5 Attach four pieces J to the cardstock at the top of the page, as shown.

6 Attach the specified photos (photos 3) to the appropriate areas, centering them on the mats.

Tip & Technique
Circle Punches

Journaling Idea
For a fun title, use a word and its definition.

For full recipe and Tip & Technique see index pg. 125

© 2005 JRL PUBLICATIONS

[de · light]

to give great pleasure

2005

It is a small world after all! Just look at the friends we made at Disneyland.

.... Cutting Instructions ....

B&T Paper

G 4 x 6	G 4 x 6

E 3 x 3	A 3 x 4

J — 2" Circle

F — 2" Circle   SCRAP

Cardstock

B
6 x 12

1 1 x 12

SCRAP

Cardstock

C 4 x 6	H 4 x 6

D
3 x 9

SCRAP

© 2005 JRL PUBLICATIONS

D R A M A T I C   F A S H I O N VARIOUS ELEMENTS COMBINE TO CREATE DRAMATIC FASHION

.... Cutting Instructions ....

B&T Paper

A 7 x 2	**M** 7 x 2

K 1 x 3

SCRAP

B&T Paper

E 2 x 7

I 5 x 2

SCRAP

Cardstock

G 4-1/4 x 4-1/4	**G** 4-1/4 x 4-1/4	**B** 1-1/2 x 1-1/2
P 6-1/4 x 4-1/4	**O** 4-1/4 x 4-1/4	
	H 1-1/2 x 4-1/4	

SCRAP

Cardstock

F 1-1/2 x 1-1/2

C 7 x 5	**L** 7 x 5

SCRAP

D 3 x 7	**J** 5 x 5

SCRAP

N 1-1/2 x 1-1/2

© 2005 JRL PUBLICATIONS

Layout Materials

12" x 12" Base Cardstock (2)
12" x 12" Cardstock (2)
12" x 12" B&T Paper (2)

Left Page Dimensions

A 7" x 2"
B 1-1/2" x 1-1/2"
C 7" x 5"
D 3" x 7"
E 2" x 7"
F 1-1/2" x 1-1/2" (3)
G 4-1/4" x 4-1/4" (2)
H 1-1/2" x 4-1/4"

Right Page Dimensions

I 5" x 2"
J 5" x 5"
K 1" x 3"
L 7" x 5"
M 7" x 2"
N 1-1/2" x 1-1/2" (3)
O 4-1/4" x 4-1/4"
P 6-1/4" x 4-1/4"

Photo Suggestions

1 6" x 4" (3)
2 4" x 4" (3)

Suggested Title

1 1-1/2" x 6"

Suggested Journaling

1 4" x 4"

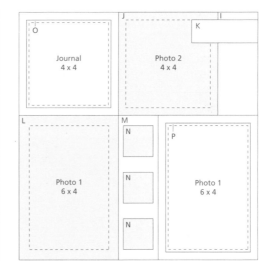

1 Using one 12" x 12" cardstock as your base, attach piece A to the top left corner of the page, keeping the edges flush.

2 Attach piece B to the top of piece A, 1" from the top edge and centered side to side.

3 Attach piece C to the top of the page next to piece A, keeping the edges flush.

4 Attach piece D to the bottom right corner of the page, keeping the edges flush.

5 Attach piece E to the bottom right of the page directly above piece C, keeping the edges flush.

6 Attach three pieces F directly to piece E, centered horizontally and spaced evenly.

7 Attach one piece G to the bottom left of the page, 3/8" from the left and bottom edges.

8 Attach remaining piece G to cardstock base at the top right of the page, 3/8" from the right side and 3/8" from pieces C and E.

9 Attach piece H to the top right of the page 1/4" above piece G, keeping 3/8" from the sides of the page.

10 Attach the specified photos (photos 1-2) to the appropriate areas, centering them on the mats.

1 Using one 12" x 12" cardstock as your base, attach piece I to the top right corner of the page, keeping the edges flush.

2 Attach piece J to the left of piece I, keeping the edges flush.

3 Attach piece K to the top right of the page directly on piece I and J, 1/2" from the top of the page, keeping the right edges flush.

4 Attach piece L to the bottom left corner of the page, keeping the edges flush.

5 Attach piece M to the right of piece L, keeping the edges flush.

6 Attach three pieces N directly to piece M, centered vertically and spaced evenly.

7 Center piece O to cardstock base on the top left corner of the page.

8 Center piece P to cardstock base on the bottom right corner of the page.

9 Attach the specified photos (photos 1-2) to the appropriate areas, centering them on the mats.

Tip & Technique
Combining accents

Journaling Idea
Round one edge of your journaling box to give it a tag-like appearance.

For full recipe and Tip & Technique see index pg. 125

© 2005 JRL PUBLICATIONS

Form & Function

Layout Materials

12" x 12" Base Cardstock (2)
12" x 12" Cardstock (4)
12" x 12" B&T Paper (2)

Left Page Dimensions

A 4" x 4"
B 8" x 4"
C 6" x 8"
D 4-1/2" x 6-1/2"
E 2" x 2"
F 2" x 2"
G 2" x 2"
H 2" x 2"
I 4" x 4"
J 4" x 4"

Right Page Dimensions

K 6" x 8"
L 8" x 4"
M 2" x 8"
N 6-1/2" x 4-1/2" (2)
O 4" x 12"

Photo Suggestions

1 4" x 6"
2 3" x 3" (3)
3 6" x 4" (2)

Suggested Title

1 3-1/2" x 11-1/2"

Suggested Journaling

1 7" x 3"

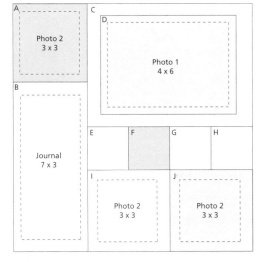

Left page layout: A Photo 2 3 x 3, B, C, D Photo 1 4 x 6, E, F, G, H, Journal 7 x 3, I Photo 2 3 x 3, J Photo 2 3 x 3

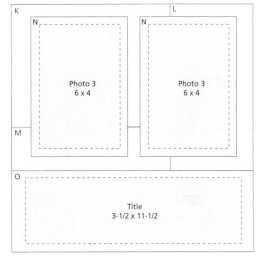

Right page layout: K, L, N Photo 3 6 x 4, N Photo 3 6 x 4, M, O Title 3-1/2 x 11-1/2

1 Using one 12" x 12" cardstock as your base, attach piece A to the top left corner of the page, keeping the edges flush.

2 Attach piece B to the bottom left corner of the page, keeping the edges flush.

3 Attach piece C to the top right corner of the page, keeping the edges flush.

4 Attach piece D to the center of piece C.

5 Attach pieces E, F, G, and H across the page directly under piece C, keeping the edges flush.

6 Attach piece I to the bottom of the page, placing it to the right of piece B, keeping the edges flush.

7 Attach piece J to the bottom right corner of the page, keeping the edges flush.

8 Attach the specified photos (photos 1-2) to the appropriate areas, centering them on the mats.

1 Using one 12" x 12" cardstock as your base, attach piece K to the top left corner of the page, keeping the edges flush.

2 Attach piece L to the top right corner of the page, keeping the edges flush.

3 Attach piece M directly under piece K, keeping the edges flush.

4 Attach the two pieces N to pieces K, L, and M, placing them 3/4" from the top of the page, 1" from the left side of the page, and 1/2" apart.

5 Attach piece O to the bottom of the page, keeping edges flush.

6 Attach the specified photos (photos 3) to the appropriate areas, centering them on the mats.

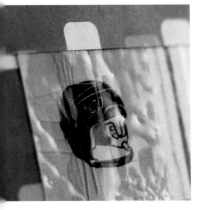

Tip & Technique
Cracked glass

Journaling Idea
Anchor journaling with coordinating accents in groups of three.

For full recipe and Tip & Technique see index pg. 125

B&T Paper

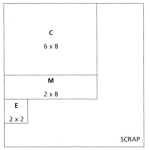

C 6 x 8

M 2 x 8

E 2 x 2

SCRAP

© 2005 JRL PUBLICATIONS

Cutting Instructions

B&T Paper

K 6 x 8	I 4 x 4
	G 2 x 2
SCRAP	

Cardstock

		H 2 x 2
B 8 x 4	L 8 x 4	
		SCRAP

Cardstock*

O 4 x 12	
N 6-1/2 x 4-1/2	N 6-1/2 x 4-1/2
	SCRAP

Cardstock*

D 4-1/2 x 6-1/2	J 4 x 4
	SCRAP

Cardstock

A 4 x 4	F 2 x 2
	SCRAP

© 2005 JRL PUBLICATIONS

*Identical papers

adore

"IN THE PAGES OF MY SCRAPBOOK,
BABIES STAY BABIES FOREVER."

October 12, 2004
Each year Sarah and Johnny look forward to going to Grandpa's farm and finding the perfect pumpkin. This year we took pictures to capture the moment. We had so much fun that Sarah said, "Mom, we should do this everyday." I remember feeling the same excitement when I was a child. It is amazing to see how traditions are carried down for generations.

GRANDPA'S
Pumpkin patch

thankful hearts

fall treasures

RISE TO THE OCCASION THIS PAGE DESIGN HELPS YOUR STORIES RISE TO THE OCCASION

.... Cutting Instructions ....

Cardstock

| B 6 x 7-1/2 | |
| I 6 x 6 | SCRAP |

Cardstock

	J 6 x 6
A 12 x 4-1/2	
	SCRAP

B&T Paper

| G 6 x 9 | |
| D 6 x 7-1/2 | SCRAP |

Cardstock

C 4-1/2 x 6-1/4	H 4-1/2 x 6-1/4	F 6 x 3
E 3-1/2 X 7-1/2		
		SCRAP

© 2005 JRL PUBLICATIONS

Layout Materials

12" x 12" Base Cardstock (2)
12" x 12" Cardstock (3)
12" x 12" B&T Paper (1)

Left Page Dimensions

A 12" x 4-1/2"
B 6" x 7-1/2"
C 4-1/2" x 6-1/4"
D 6" x 7-1/2"
E 3-1/2" x 7-1/2"

Right Page Dimensions

F 6" x 3"
G 6" x 9"
H 4-1/2" x 6-1/4"
I 6" x 6"
J 6" x 6"

Photo Suggestions

1 5-1/4" x 3-1/2" (3)
2 3-1/2" x 5-1/4" (2)
3 2-1/2" x 2-1/2" (2)

Suggested Title

1 3" x 7"

Suggested Journaling

1 5-1/2" x 2-1/2"

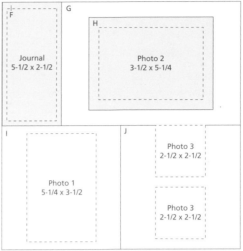

LEFT

A
B
C — Photo 2 3-1/2 x 5-1/4
Photo 1 5-1/4 x 3-1/2
D
E — Title 3 x 7
Photo 1 5-1/4 x 3-1/2

RIGHT

F — Journal 5-1/2 x 2-1/2
G
H — Photo 2 3-1/2 x 5-1/4
I — Photo 1 5-1/4 x 3-1/2
J — Photo 3 2-1/2 x 2-1/2 / Photo 3 2-1/2 x 2-1/2

LEFT

1 Using one 12" x 12" cardstock as your base, attach piece A to the left side of the page, keeping the edges flush.

2 Attach piece B to the top right corner of the page, keeping the edges flush.

3 Attach piece C to the center of piece B.

4 Attach piece D to the bottom right corner of the page, keeping the side edges flush.

5 Attach piece E to the center of piece D, placing it 1-1/2" from the top and bottom of piece D, keeping the side edges flush.

6 Attach the specified photos (photos 1-2) to the appropriate areas, centering them on the mats.

RIGHT

1 Using one 12" x 12" cardstock as your base, attach piece F to the top left corner of the page, keeping the edges flush.

2 Attach piece G to the top right corner of the page, keeping the edges flush.

3 Attach piece H to the center of piece G, 3/4" from the top and bottom edge and 1-1/4" from the left and right edges.

4 Attach piece I to the bottom left corner of the page, keeping the edges flush.

5 Attach piece J to the bottom right corner of the page, keeping the edges flush.

6 Attach the specified photos (photos 1-3) to the appropriate areas, centering them on the mats.

Tip & Technique
Paper tearing

Journaling Idea
When writing about a tradition, include thoughts and specific details.

For full recipe and Tip & Technique see index pg. 126

© 2005 JRL PUBLICATIONS

Scenic Byway

Layout Materials

12" x 12" Base Cardstock (2)
12" x 12" Cardstock (1)
12" x 12" B&T Paper (1)

Left Page Dimensions

A 4-1/2" x 12"
B 4" x 6"

Right Page Dimensions

C 9-1/2" x 12
D 4" x 6"

Photo Suggestions

1 4" oval (2)
2 3" circle (4)
3 2" x 2"
4 3" x 3"
5 4" x 4"

Suggested Title

1 2" x 19"

Suggested Journaling

1 4" x 4"

LEFT

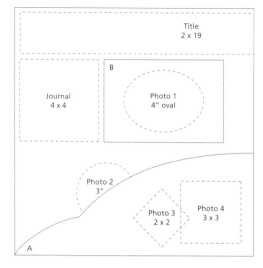

Title
2 x 19

B

Journal
4 x 4

Photo 1
4" oval

Photo 2
3"

Photo 3
2 x 2

Photo 4
3 x 3

A

RIGHT

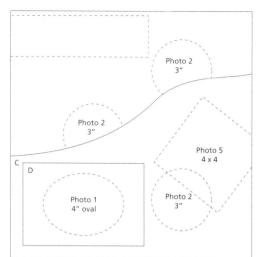

Photo 2
3"

Photo 2
3"

Photo 5
4 x 4

C

D

Photo 1
4" oval

Photo 2
3"

1 Gently cut or tear piece A, beginning 4-1/2" from the top left corner and ending 1/2" from the top right corner as shown

2 Using one 12" x 12" cardstock as your base, attach piece A to the bottom of the page, keeping the edges flush.

3 Attach piece B 2-1/2" from the top of the page and 1-1/2" from the right side of the page.

4 Attach the specified photos (photos 1-4) to the appropriate areas.

1 Gently cut or tear piece C from the remaining cardstock, beginning 4-1/2" from the bottom left corner and ending 9-1/2" from the bottom right corner as shown

2 Using one 12" x 12" cardstock as your base, attach piece C to the bottom of the page, keeping the edges flush.

3 Attach piece D to the bottom left side of the page directly on piece C, 1/2" from the side and bottom edge of the page.

4 Attach the specified photos (photos 1, 2, and 5) to the appropriate areas.

Tip & Technique
Fun Flock

Journaling Idea
When space permits, use a large title over two pages.

For full recipe and Tip & Technique see index pg. 126

© 2005 JRL PUBLICATIONS

Cutting Instructions

B&T Paper

D	B
4 x 6	4 x 6

SCRAP

Cardstock

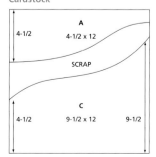

A
4-1/2 x 12
4-1/2

SCRAP

C
4-1/2   9-1/2 x 12   9-1/2

© 2005 JRL PUBLICATIONS

Boys will be boys! Parker and Cooper love the outdoors. They loved playing on this old wagon in the field behind my friends house. Parker also loved some time on the swing.

Brothers

Cooper

Parker

HARMONIOUS PATTERNS PATTERNS OF PHOTOS AND STRIPS OF ACCENTS SHOW OFF WELL

.... *Cutting Instructions* ....

B&T Paper

H 6 x 3	H 6 x 3	M 6 x 2	C 6 x 4
A 4 x 6			SCRAP

B&T Paper

L 6 x 4	D 6 x 2
	SCRAP

Cardstock

F 1 x 6
F 1 x 6
K — 1-1/2 Circle
K — 1-1/2 Circle
K — 1-1/2 Circle

SCRAP

Cardstock

E 3 x 6	
E 3 x 6	
B 2 x 6	
I 4 x 6	SCRAP

Cardstock

G 4-1/2 x 4-1/2	N 4-1/2 x 4-1/2
J 2 x 6	
	SCRAP

© 2005 JRL PUBLICATIONS

Layout Materials

12" x 12" Base Cardstock (2)
12" x 12" Cardstock (3)
12" x 12" B&T Paper (2)

Left Page Dimensions

A 4" x 6"
B 2" x 6"
C 6" x 4"
D 6" x 2"
E 3" x 6" (2)
F 1" x 6" (2)
G 4-1/2" x 4-1/2"

Right Page Dimensions

H 6" x 3" (2)
I 4" x 6"
J 2" x 6"
K 1-1/2" circle (3)
L 6" x 4"
M 6" x 2"
N 4-1/2" x 4-1/2"

Photo Suggestions

1 3" x 5"
2 4" x 4" (4)

Suggested Title

1 1-1/2" x 5-1/2"

Suggested Journaling

1 3" x 5"

LEFT

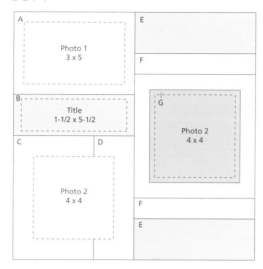

RIGHT

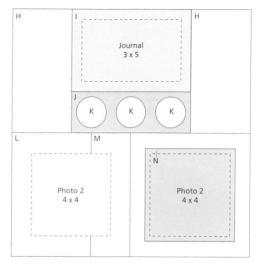

1 Using one 12" x 12" cardstock as your base, attach piece A to the top left corner of the page, keeping the edges flush.

2 Attach piece B to the left side of the page, directly below piece A, keeping the edges flush.

3 Attach piece C to the bottom left corner of the page, keeping the edges flush.

4 Attach piece D to the bottom of the page, directly to the right of piece C, keeping the edges flush.

5 Attach pieces E to the top and bottom right corners of the page, keeping the edges flush.

6 Attach one piece F to the bottom of upper piece E. Attach the other piece F to the top of lower piece E.

7 Attach piece G directly to the cardstock, 3/4" from the bottom of piece F and from the right edge of the page.

8 Attach the specified photos (photos 1-2) to the appropriate areas, centering them on the mats.

1 Using one 12" x 12" cardstock as your base, attach pieces H to the top left and right corners of the page, keeping the edges flush.

2 Attach piece I to the top center of the page, keeping the side edges flush with pieces H.

3 Attach piece J directly below piece I, keeping the edges flush.

4 Attach three K pieces horizontally on piece J, spacing them evenly.

5 Attach piece L to the bottom left corner of the page, keeping the edges flush.

6 Attach piece M to the bottom of the page, directly to the right of piece L, keeping the edges flush.

7 Attach piece N directly to the cardstock, 3/4" from the right and bottom sides of the page.

8 Attach the specified photos (photos 2) to the appropriate areas, centering them on the mats.

Tip & Technique
Sanding buttons

Journaling Idea
Quickly identify who is in each picture by placing name accents by photos.

For full recipe and Tip & Technique see index pg. 126

© 2005 JRL PUBLICATIONS

Layout Materials

12" x 12" Base Cardstock (2)
12" x 12" Cardstock (2)
12" x 12" B&T Paper (2)

Left Page Dimensions

A 12" x 6"
B 12" x 6"
C 1-1/2" x 6"
D 7" x 7"
E 3/4" x 7"

Right Page Dimensions

F 2" x 12"
G 4" x 12"
H 1-1/2" x 12"
I 6" x 12"
J 6" x 4"

Photo Suggestions

1 3" x 3" (4)
2 7" x 7"
3 4" x 6" (2)

Suggested Title/Journaling

1 3-1/2" x 5"

LEFT

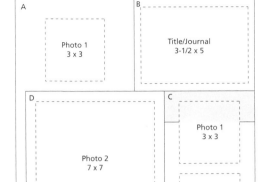

A

Photo 1
3 x 3

B

Title/Journal
3-1/2 x 5

D

Photo 2
7 x 7

E

C

Photo 1
3 x 3

Photo 1
3 x 3

RIGHT

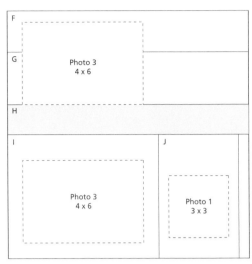

F

G

Photo 3
4 x 6

H

I

Photo 3
4 x 6

J

Photo 1
3 x 3

LEFT

1 Using one 12" x 12" cardstock as your base, attach piece A to the left side of the page, keeping the edges flush.

2 Attach piece B to the right side of the page, keeping the right edges flush.

3 Attach piece C to the bottom left of piece B, 4-1/2" from the top edge of the page, keeping the right edges flush.

4 Attach piece D to the bottom left corner of piece A, 1/2" from the left and bottom edges of the page.

5 Attach piece E to the bottom of piece D, placing it 1" from the bottom, keeping the edges flush.

6 Attach the specified photos (photos 1-2) to the appropriate areas, centering them on the mats.

RIGHT

1 Using one 12" x 12" cardstock as your base, attach piece F to the top left of the page, keeping the edges flush.

2 Attach piece G directly below piece F, keeping the edges flush.

3 Attach piece H to the bottom of piece G, keeping the edges flush. Make sure piece H lines up with piece C on the left page.

4 Attach piece I to the bottom left of the page, keeping the edges flush.

5 Attach piece J to piece I, 1/2" from the right side, keeping the edges flush.

6 Attach the specified photos (photos 1 and 3) to the appropriate areas, centering them on the mats.

Tip & Technique
Staples

Journaling Idea
Adhesive tags are ideal for adding journal entries.

For full recipe and Tip & Technique see index pg. 126

© 2005 JRL PUBLICATIONS

OUR CAMP

Scout Camp '04
Bear Lake, Utah
What an adventure!!

Survival Skills

PLEASING PARADIGM PLACE PROMINENT PIECES TO CREATE A PLEASING PARADIGM

.... *Cutting Instructions* ....

Cardstock

A 12 x 6	F 2 x 12	
		SCRAP

Cardstock

B 12 x 6	I 6 x 12

B&T Paper

G 4 x 12	
D 7 x 7	J 6 x 4
	SCRAP

B&T Paper

H 1-1/2 x 12
E 3/4 x 7
C 1-1/2 x 6

SCRAP

© 2005 JRL PUBLICATIONS

PHOTO FUSION   CREATE VISUAL FUSION WITH THIS FUN LAYOUT FOR VARIED PHOTOS

.... *Cutting Instructions* ....

Cardstock

| G |
| 3-1/2 x 7 |

| A |
| 5 x 3-1/2 |

SCRAP

B&T Paper

| C | E |
| 7 x 7 | 7 x 5 |

SCRAP

Cardstock

| D |
| 6 x 6 |

H 2-1/2 x 2-1/2

B 12 x 1-1/2
F 1-1/2 x 12

SCRAP

© 2005 JRL PUBLICATIONS

Layout Materials

12" x 12" Base Cardstock (2)
12" x 12" Cardstock (2)
12" x 12" B&T Paper (1)

Left Page Dimensions

A　5" x 3-1/2"
B　12" x 1-1/2"
C　7" x 7"
D　6" x 6"

Right Page Dimensions

E　7" x 5"
F　1-1/2" x 12"
G　3-1/2" x 7"
H　2-1/2" x 2-1/2"

Photo Suggestions

1　2-1/2" x 2-1/2"
2　3-1/2" x 5"
3　5" x 5"
4　5" x 3-1/2"
5　4" x 3" (2)

Suggested Title

1　2" x 6"

Suggested Journaling

1　7" x 2-1/2"

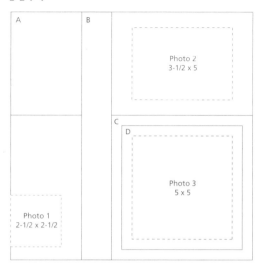

A
B
Photo 2
3-1/2 x 5
C
D
Photo 3
5 x 5
Photo 1
2-1/2 x 2-1/2

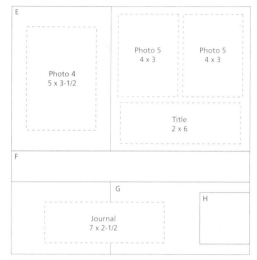

E
Photo 5
4 x 3
Photo 5
4 x 3
Photo 4
5 x 3-1/2
Title
2 x 6
F
G
H
Journal
7 x 2-1/2

1　Using one 12" x 12" cardstock as your base, attach piece A to the top left corner of the page, keeping the edges flush.

2　Attach one piece B along the right side of piece A, keeping the edges flush.

3　Attach piece C to the right bottom corner of the page, keeping the edges flush.

4　Attach piece D to the center of piece C.

5　Attach the specified photos (photos 1-3) to the appropriate areas, centering them on the mats.

1　Using one 12" x 12" cardstock as your base, attach piece E to the top left corner of the page, keeping the edges flush.

2　Attach piece F horizontally along the bottom of piece E, keeping the edges flush.

3　Attach piece G to bottom right corner of the page, keeping the edges flush.

4　Attach piece H to the bottom right corner of piece G, 1/2" from top and bottom of piece G, keeping the right edges flush.

5　Attach the specified photos (photos 4-5) to the appropriate areas, centering them on the mats.

Photo Fusion

Tip & Technique
Paper piecing

Journaling Idea
Be creative by breaking up the journaling space.

For full recipe and Tip & Technique see index pg. 126

© 2005 JRL PUBLICATIONS

Gallery Collection

Layout Materials

12" x 12" Base Cardstock (2)
12" x 12" Cardstock (3)
12" x 12" B&T Paper (2)

Left Page Dimensions

A 4-1/2" x 4-1/2"
B 4-1/2" x 6-1/2"
C 6-1/2" x 4-1/2"
D 6-1/2" x 4-1/2"
E 6-1/2" x 2"

Right Page Dimensions

F 4-1/2" x 4-1/2"
G 4-1/2" x 4-1/2"
H 2" x 9-1/4"
I 4-1/2" x 4-1/2"
J 4-1/2" x 4-1/2"
K 11-1/2" x 2"

Photo Suggestions

1 4" x 6"
2 6" x 4" (2)
3 4" x 4" (5)

Suggested Title

1 1-1/2" x 8-3/4"

Suggested Journaling

1 10" x 1-1/2"

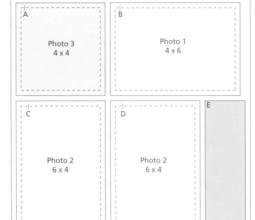

Left page layout:
- A — Photo 3, 4 x 4
- B — Photo 1, 4 x 6
- C — Photo 2, 6 x 4
- D — Photo 2, 6 x 4
- E

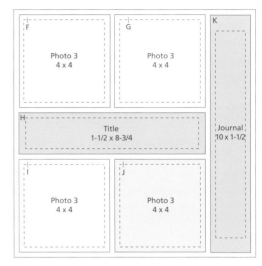

Right page layout:
- F — Photo 3, 4 x 4
- G — Photo 3, 4 x 4
- K — Journal, 10 x 1-1/2
- H — Title, 1-1/2 x 8-3/4
- I — Photo 3, 4 x 4
- J — Photo 3, 4 x 4

LEFT

1 Using one 12" x 12" cardstock as your base, attach piece A to the top left side of the page, placing it approximately 1/4" from the top and left edges.

2 Attach piece B to the top right of the page, placing it approximately 1/4" from the top and right edges.

3 Attach piece C to the bottom left corner of the page, placing it approximately 1/4" from the bottom and left edges.

4 Attach piece D 1/4" to the right of piece C and 1/4" from the bottom edge.

5 Attach piece E to the bottom right of the page, placing it approximately 1/4" from the bottom and right edges.

6 Attach the specified photos (photos 1-2) to the appropriate areas, centering them on the mats.

RIGHT

1 Using one 12" x 12" cardstock as your base, attach piece F to the top left corner of the page, placing it approximately 1/4" from the left and top edges.

2 Attach piece G to the top of the page 1/4" to the right of piece F, and 1/4" from the top edge.

3 Attach piece H across the center of the page, placing it approximately 1/4" from the left edge and from pieces F and G.

4 Attach piece I to the bottom left side of the page, placing it approximately 1/4" from the left and bottom edges, and from piece H.

5 Attach piece J to the bottom of the page, placing it approximately 1/4" from the bottom edge and from pieces H and I.

6 Attach piece K to the right side of the page, placing it approximately 1/4" from the outside edges and pieces G, H, and J.

7 Attach the specified photos (photos 3) to the appropriate areas, centering them on the mats.

Tip & Technique

Rotate concept to complement photos

Journaling Idea

Tear the edges of your journaling boxes to give them a rugged look.

For full recipe and Tip & Technique see index pg. 127

© 2005 JRL PUBLICATIONS

In this family, you gotta learn young to ride a four wheeler and generally rough it! We've learned that the time we spend together is some of the best times we've had. And we know the memories will last forever. This year Dad bought us each a four wheeler, and every Saturday, off we go!

.... *Cutting Instructions* ....

Cardstock

D
6-1/2 x 4-1/2

G
4-1/2 x 4-1/2

SCRAP

Cardstock

B
4-1/2 x 6-1/2

I
4-1/2 x 4-1/2

SCRAP

Cardstock

C
6-1/2 x 4-1/2

F
4-1/2 x 4-1/2

SCRAP

B&T Paper

A
4-1/2 x 4-1/2

J
4-1/2 x 4-1/2

SCRAP

B&T Paper

H 2 x 9-1/4

E 6-1/2 x 2

K 11-1/2 x 2

SCRAP

© 2005 JRL PUBLICATIONS

THEN & NOW BRING PHOTOS OF THE PAST INTO THE PRESENT WITH A GREAT DESIGN CONCEPT

Cutting Instructions

B&T Paper

L 1 x 7

A 12 x 1-1/2

SCRAP

B&T Paper

D
8 x 6

C 12 x 1-1/2

H 1-1/2 x 12

M
4 x 5

SCRAP

B&T Paper

I
6-1/2 x 12

B 12 x 1-1/2

E 1 x 6

SCRAP

Cardstock

J 1 x 4-1/2

G 1 x 3-1/2

F
5 x 7

K
5 x 7

SCRAP

© 2005 JRL PUBLICATIONS

Layout Materials

12" x 12" Base Cardstock (2)
12" x 12" Cardstock (1)
12" x 12" B&T Paper (3)

Left Page
Dimensions

A **12" x 1-1/2"**
B **12" x 1-1/2"**
C **12" x 1-1/2"**
D **8" x 6"**
E **1" x 6"**
F **5" x 7"**
G **1" x 3-1/2"**

Right Page
Dimensions

H **1-1/2" x 12"**
I **6-1/2" x 12"**
J **1" x 4-1/2"**
K **5" x 7"**
L **1" x 7"**
M **4" x 5"**

Photo
Suggestions

1 **4" x 3"**
2 **4" x 6"** (2)
3 **3" x 4"** (2)

Suggested Title

1 **2" x 13-1/2"**

Suggested
Journaling

1 **1" x 3"**

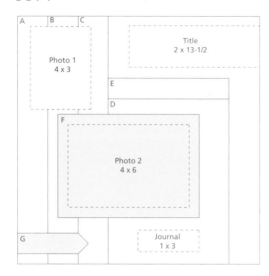

Title
2 x 13-1/2

Photo 1
4 x 3

E

D

F

Photo 2
4 x 6

G

Journal
1 x 3

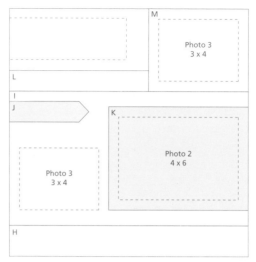

M

Photo 3
3 x 4

L

I

J

K

Photo 3
3 x 4

Photo 2
4 x 6

H

1 Using one 12" x 12" cardstock as your base, attach piece A to the left side of the page, keeping the edges flush.

2 Attach piece B to the right of piece A, keeping the edges flush.

3 Attach piece C to the right of piece B, keeping the edges flush.

4 Attach piece D to the bottom of the page, to the right of piece C, keeping the edges flush.

5 Attach piece E above piece D, keeping the edges flush.

6 Attach piece F on top of pieces B, C, and D, 5" from the top and 2" from the left side of the page.

7 Trim piece G into a tag and attach to the lower left, placing it 1/2" from the bottom and keeping the left edges flush.

8 Attach the specified photos (photos 1-2) to the appropriate areas, centering them on the mats.

1 Using one 12" x 12" cardstock as your base, attach piece H to the bottom of the page, keeping the edges flush.

2 Attach piece I across the center of the page, directly above piece H, keeping the edges flush.

3 Trim piece J into a tag and attach to the left side of piece I, placing it 1/2" from the top of piece I, keeping the left edges flush.

4 Attach piece K on the right side of piece I, placing it 3/4" from the top, keeping the right edges flush.

5 Attach piece L to the left side of the page, placing it above piece I, keeping edges flush.

6 Attach piece M to the top right corner of the page, keeping the edges flush.

7 Attach the specified photos (photos 2-3) to the appropriate areas, centering them on the mats.

Then & Now

Tip & Technique
Sassy Strands™

Journaling Idea
If your journaling requires additional space, simply increase the size of your journaling box.

For full recipe and Tip & Technique see index pg. 127

© 2005 JRL PUBLICATIONS

Layout Materials

12" x 12" Base Cardstock (2)
12" x 12" Cardstock (2)
12" x 12" B&T Paper (2)

Left Page Dimensions

A 8" x 4-1/2"
B 8" x 4-1/2"
C 1-1/2" circle (3)
D 1-1/2" x 9"
E 1/2" x 9"
F 12" x 3"
G 2-1/2" x 2-1/2"

Right Page Dimensions

H 12" x 6"
I 12" x 6"
J 7" x 5"
K 1-1/2" x 6"
L 1/2" x 6"
M 1-1/2" circle

Photo Suggestions

1 5" x 3-1/2" (2)
2 2" x 2"
3 3-1/2" x 5" (2)
4 6" x 4"

Suggested Title

1 1-1/2" x 8"

Suggested Journaling

1 6-1/2" x 2-1/2"

LEFT

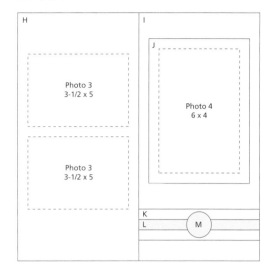

- Title 1-1/2 x 8
- F
- G Photo 2 2 x 2
- D
- E
- A
- B
- Photo 1 5 x 3-1/2
- Photo 1 5 x 3-1/2
- Journal 6-1/2 x 2-1/2
- C C C

RIGHT

- H
- I
- J
- Photo 3 3-1/2 x 5
- Photo 4 6 x 4
- Photo 3 3-1/2 x 5
- K
- L M

Left

1 Using one 12" x 12" cardstock as your base, attach piece A to the bottom left corner of the page, keeping the edges flush.

2 Attach piece B to the right of piece A, keeping the edges flush.

3 Attach pieces C to the bottom of pieces A and B, 1/2" from the bottom of the page and 1" from each other or as desired.

4 Attach piece D above pieces A and B, keeping the edges flush.

5 Attach piece E to the center of piece D, keeping the side edges flush.

6 Attach piece F to the right side of the page, keeping the edges flush.

7 Attach piece G to piece F, 1/4" from the top and right edges of the page.

8 Attach the specified photos (photos 1-2) to the appropriate areas, centering them on the mats.

Right

1 Using one 12" x 12" cardstock as your base, attach piece H to the left side of the page, keeping the edges flush.

2 Attach piece I to the right side of the page, keeping the edges flush.

3 Attach piece J to piece I, 1-1/4" from top edge and 1/2" from left and right edges.

4 Attach piece K to the bottom of piece I, placing it 1" from the bottom, keeping the side edges flush.

5 Attach piece L to the center of piece K, keeping the side edges flush.

6 Attach piece M to pieces K and L as shown.

7 Attach the specified photos (photos 3-4) to the appropriate areas, centering them on the mats.

Tip & Technique
Liquid Glass

Journaling Idea
For a fun accent, random stamp your own B&T paper with words that describe the event.

For full recipe and Tip & Technique see index pg. 127

© 2005 JRL PUBLICATIONS

our little...

Love Bug

She is our little love bug

March 13th, 2006

Emilyn did not used to like to get her picture taken. then one day she decided it was kind of fun. Now she loves to pose for the camera. She is such a sweetie and is growing up so fast. I love to see her become more independent

sweet

C L E A R   D I M E N S I O N   CLEAR DIMENSION ACCENTUATES YOUR ARTWORK IN A STRAIGHTFORWARD DESIGN

··········· *Cutting Instructions* ··

B&T Paper

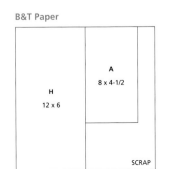

H
12 x 6

A
8 x 4-1/2

B&T Paper

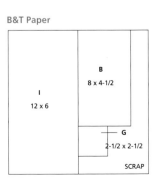

I
12 x 6

B
8 x 4-1/2

G
2-1/2 x 2-1/2

SCRAP

Cardstock

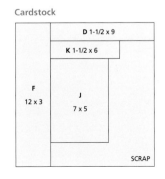

D 1-1/2 x 9

K 1-1/2 x 6

F
12 x 3

J
7 x 5

SCRAP

Cardstock

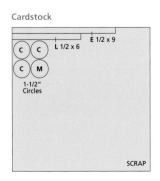

E 1/2 x 9

L 1/2 x 6

C C

C M

1-1/2"
Circles

SCRAP

© 2005 JRL PUBLICATIONS

BALANCED BLOCKS A TRUE BALANCE OF BLOCKS MAKES AN ATTRACTIVE LAYOUT

.... *Cutting Instructions* ....

Cardstock

G 4 x 5-1/2	B 3 x 3
G 4 x 5-1/2	B 3 x 3
E 4 x 5-1/2	SCRAP

Cardstock

D 6-1/2 x 4-1/2	J 6-1/2 x 4-1/2
C 3 x 6	
F H H	2-1/2 x 2-1/2 SCRAP

B&T Paper

A 8 X 12	I 12 x 3	SCRAP

© 2005 JRL PUBLICATIONS

Layout Materials

12" x 12" Base Cardstock (2)
12" x 12" Cardstock (2)
12" x 12" B&T Paper (1)

Left Page Dimensions

A 8" x 12"
B 3" x 3" (2)
C 3" x 6"
D 6-1/2" x 4-1/2"
E 4" x 5-1/2"
F 2-1/2" x 2-1/2"

Right Page Dimensions

G 4" x 5-1/2" (2)
H 2-1/2" x 2-1/2" (2)
I 12" x 3"
J 6-1/2" x 4-1/2"

Photo Suggestions

1 6" x 4" (2)
2 3-1/2" x 5" (2)
3 2" x 2"

Suggested Title

1 2" x 5"

Suggested Journaling

1 3-1/2" x 5"

LEFT

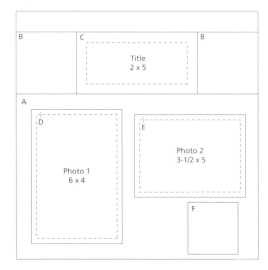

RIGHT

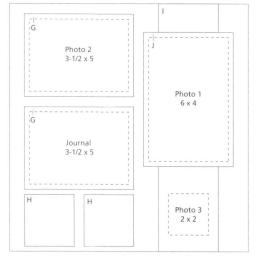

LEFT

1 Using one 12" x 12" cardstock as your base, attach piece A to the bottom of the page, keeping the edges flush.

2 Attach one piece B to the left side of the page, directly on top of piece A, keeping the left side edges flush.

3 Attach piece C to the center of the page, directly on top of piece A, next to piece B, keeping the edges flush.

4 Attach the second piece B to the right side of the page, directly on top of piece A, next to piece C, keeping the edges flush.

5 Attach piece D to piece A, placing it 3/4" from the left and 3/4" from the bottom edge.

6 Attach piece E to piece A, placing it 3/4" from the right and 1" from the top of piece A.

7 Attach piece F to the bottom right page, placing it 3/4" from the right edge and 1/4" from the bottom.

8 Attach the specified photos (photos 1-2) and desired accents to the appropriate areas, centering them on the mats.

RIGHT

1 Using one 12" x 12" cardstock as your base, attach one piece G to the top left side of the page, placing it 1/2" from the top and right edges; add second piece G 1/4" below and 1/2" from the right edge of the page.

2 Attach the two piece H squares to the bottom of the page, placing them 1/2" from the left, 1/4" from the bottom, and 1/2" from each other.

3 Attach piece I down the right side of the page, keeping the top and bottom edges flush, placing it 1-1/2" from the right edge.

4 Attach piece J to piece I on the left side of the page, placing it 3/4" from the left and 1" from the top of the page.

5 Attach the specified photos (photos 1-3) and desired accents to the appropriate areas.

Tip & Technique
Paper crinkling

Journaling Idea
Soften your title by using all lowercase letters.

For full recipe and Tip & Technique see index pg. 127

© 2005 JRL PUBLICATIONS

Easy Inspiration

Layout Materials

12" x 12" Base Cardstock **(2)**
12" x 12" Cardstock **(2)**
12" x 12" B&T Paper **(3)**

*Left Page
Dimensions*

A **1" x 12"**
B **5" x 6"**
C **5" x 6"**
D **6" x 6"**
E **5" x 5"**
F **6" x 6"**
G **5" x 5"**

*Right Page
Dimensions*

H **1" x 12"**
I **5" x 6"**
J **3" x 6"**
K **8" x 6"**
L **3" x 3"**
M **3" x 3"**
N **3" x 6"**

*Photo
Suggestions*

1 **4" x 5" (3)**
2 **4" x 4" (2)**
3 **2-1/2" x 2-1/2"**
4 **6" x 4"**

Suggested Title

1 **2-1/2" x 5-1/2"**

*Suggested
Journaling*

1 **2-1/2" x 5-1/2"**

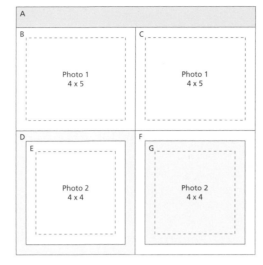

A
B | C
Photo 1 4 x 5 | Photo 1 4 x 5
D E | F G
Photo 2 4 x 4 | Photo 2 4 x 4

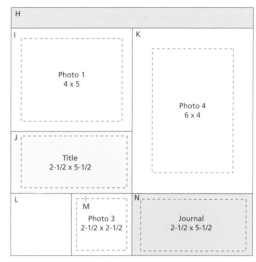

H
I | K
Photo 1 4 x 5 | Photo 4 6 x 4
J
Title 2-1/2 x 5-1/2
L | M Photo 3 2-1/2 x 2-1/2 | N Journal 2-1/2 x 5-1/2

1 Using one 12" x 12" cardstock as your base, attach piece A to the top of the page, keeping the edges flush.

2 Attach piece B to the left of the page directly under piece A, keeping the edges flush.

3 Attach piece C to the right of piece B and directly under piece A, keeping the edges flush.

4 Attach piece D to the bottom left corner of the page, keeping the edges flush.

5 Attach piece E to the center of piece D.

6 Attach piece F to the bottom right corner of the page, keeping the edges flush with pieces C and D.

7 Attach piece G to the center of piece F.

8 Attach the specified photos (photos 1-2) to the appropriate areas, centering them on the mats.

1 Using one 12" x 12" cardstock as your base, attach piece H to the top of the page, keeping the edges flush.

2 Attach piece I to the left of the page directly under piece H.

3 Attach piece J directly below piece I, keeping the edges flush.

4 Attach piece K to the right of pieces I and J, keeping the edges flush.

5 Attach piece L to the bottom left corner of the page, keeping the edges flush.

6 Attach piece M to the right of piece L, keeping the edges flush.

7 Attach piece N to the bottom right corner of the page, keeping the edges flush.

8 Attach the specified photos (photos 1, 3, and 4) to the appropriate areas, centering them on the mats.

Tip & Technique
**Accenting photos
with My Stickease™**

Journaling Idea
**Title and journaling
boxes are only
suggestions; use
the space to best
complement your
unique design.**

*For full recipe and Tip &
Technique see index pg. 127*

© 2005 JRL PUBLICATIONS

EASY INSPIRATION CLEAN AND SIMPLE LINES PROVIDE EASY INSPIRATION FOR THIS LAYOUT

.... *Cutting Instructions* ....

B&T Paper

K
8 x 6

B
5 x 6

L
3 x 3

SCRAP

B&T Paper

F
6 x 6

I
5 x 6

SCRAP

Cardstock

C
5 x 6

E
5 x 5

M
3 x 3

SCRAP

Cardstock

D
6 x 6

J
3 x 6

G
5 x 5

SCRAP

B&T Paper

A 1 x 12

H 1 x 12

N
3 x 6

SCRAP

© 2005 JRL PUBLICATIONS

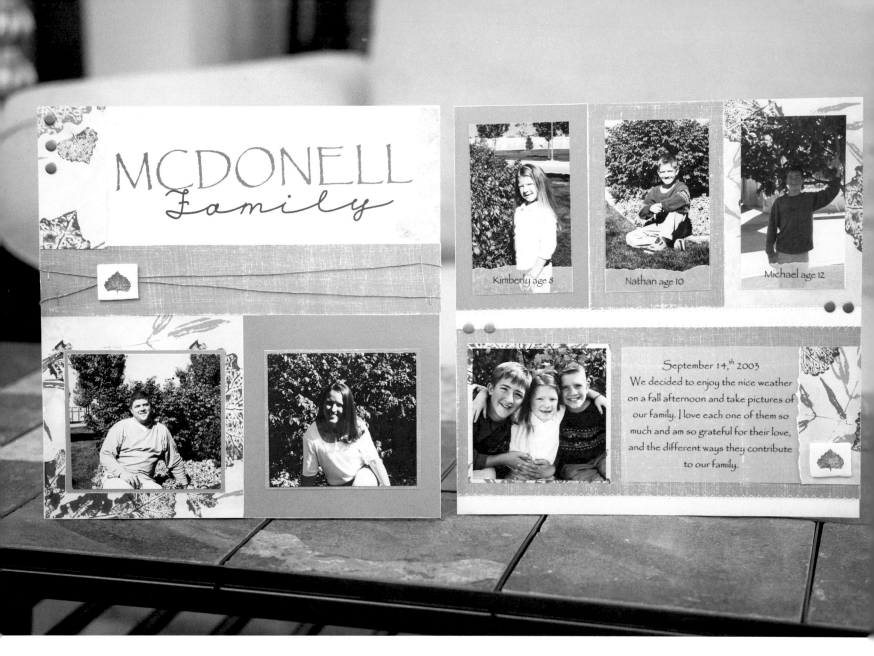

MCDONELL *Family*

Kimberly age 8

Nathan age 10

Michael age 12

September 14,th 2003
We decided to enjoy the nice weather
on a fall afternoon and take pictures of
our family. I love each one of them so
much and am so grateful for their love,
and the different ways they contribute
to our family.

RISE 'N SHINE HELP YOUR PAGES RISE AND SHINE WITH THESE GRACEFUL DIVISIONS

.... *Cutting Instructions* ....

Cardstock
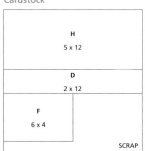

| H |
| 5 x 12 |
| D |
| 2 x 12 |
| F |
| 6 x 4 |

B&T Paper
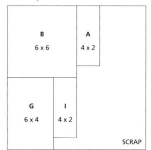

B	A
6 x 6	4 x 2
G	I
6 x 4	4 x 2
	SCRAP

Cardstock
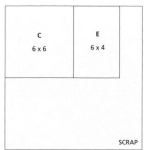

C	E
6 x 6	6 x 4
	SCRAP

© 2005 JRL PUBLICATIONS

Layout Materials

12" x 12" Base Cardstock (2)
12" x 12" Cardstock (2)
12" x 12" B&T Paper (1)

Left Page Dimensions

A 4" x 2"
B 6" x 6"
C 6" x 6"
D 2" x 12"

Right Page Dimensions

E 6" x 4"
F 6" x 4"
G 6" x 4"
H 5" x 12"
I 4" x 2"

Photo Suggestions

1 4" x 4" (3)
2 5" x 3" (3)

Suggested Title

1 2-1/2" x 9"

Suggested Journaling

1 4" x 5"

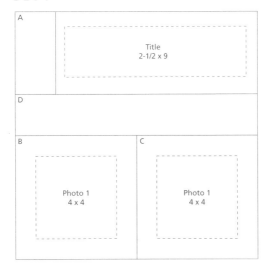

A — Title 2-1/2 x 9
D
B — Photo 1 4 x 4
C — Photo 1 4 x 4

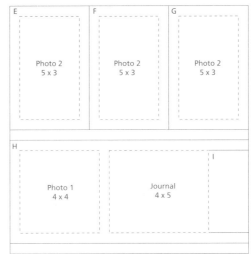

E — Photo 2 5 x 3
F — Photo 2 5 x 3
G — Photo 2 5 x 3
H — Photo 1 4 x 4
Journal 4 x 5
I

LEFT

1 Using one 12" x 12" cardstock as your base, attach piece A to the top left corner of the page, keeping the edges flush.

2 Attach piece B to the bottom left corner of the page, keeping the edges flush.

3 Attach piece C to the bottom right corner of the page, keeping the edges flush.

4 Attach piece D directly above pieces B and C, keeping the edges flush.

5 Attach the specified photos (photos 1) to the appropriate areas, centering them on the mats.

RIGHT

1 Using one 12" x 12" cardstock as your base, attach piece E to the top left corner of the page, keeping the edges flush.

2 Attach piece F to the top of the page, directly right of piece E, keeping the edges flush.

3 Attach piece G to the top right corner of the page, keeping the edges flush.

4 Attach piece H to the bottom of the page, placing it 1/2" from the bottom, keeping the edges flush.

5 Attach piece I to the right side of piece H, 1/2" from the bottom edge.

6 Attach the specified photos (photos 1-2) to the appropriate areas, centering them on the mats.

Rise 'n' Shine

Tip & Technique
Clay tiles

Journaling Idea
Soften your layout by adding journaling to vellum.

For full recipe and Tip & Technique see index pg. 127

© 2005 JRL PUBLICATIONS

Layout Materials

12" x 12" Base Cardstock (2)
12" x 12" Cardstock (4)
12" x 12" B&T Paper (1)

Left Page Dimensions

A   12" x 4-1/2"
B   6" x 7-1/2"
C   4-1/2" x 6-1/2"
D   2" x 2" (2)
E   2" x 2" (2)
F   2" x 2" (2)

Right Page Dimensions

G   6" x 12"
H   6" x 3"
I   4-1/2" x 4-1/2" (2)
J   2" x 2" (4)
K   2" x 2" (3)
L   2" x 2" (3)

Photo Suggestions

1   4" x 4" (4)
2   6" x 4"

Suggested Title/Journaling

1   2" x 4"

LEFT

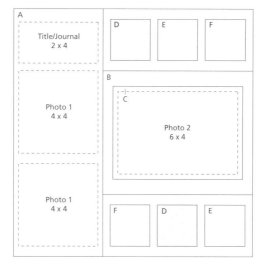

RIGHT

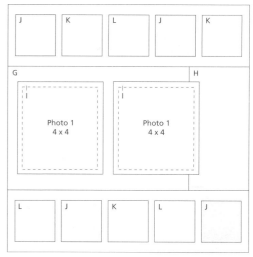

1 Using one 12" x 12" cardstock as your base, attach piece A to the left side of the page, keeping the edges flush.

2 Attach piece B to the right side of the page, placing it 3" from the top edge, keeping the side edges flush.

3 Attach piece C mat to piece B, centering it 3/4" from top and 1/2" from sides of piece B.

4 Arrange pieces D, E, and F accent squares above and below piece B, centering them horizontally, as shown. Attach and embellish as desired.

5 Attach the specified photos (photos 1-2) to the appropriate areas, centering them on the mats.

1 Using one 12" x 12" cardstock as your base, attach piece G to the center of the page, placing it 3" from the top, keeping the edges flush.

2 Attach piece H to the right of piece G, keeping the edges flush.

3 Attach pieces I to the center of pieces G and H, placing them 1/2" from the left side and each other, and 3/4" from the top of piece G.

4 Arrange pieces J, K, and L accent squares above and below piece G, centering them horizontally as shown. Attach and embellish as desired.

5 Attach the specified photos (photos 1) to the appropriate areas, centering them on the mats.

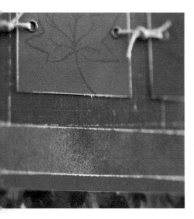

Tip & Technique
Sponged background

Journaling Idea
Adding names and ages provides a quick reference to when events took place.

For full recipe and Tip & Technique see index pg. 128

© 2005 JRL PUBLICATIONS

Discovering the Beauty of Autumn

GINO–AGE 2
OCTOBER 2004

TREASURE TAGS   A DISPLAY OF TAGS BRINGS A TREASURE OF VARIETY TO THE LAYOUT

·········· *Cutting Instructions* ··································

B&T Paper

G 6 x 12
B 6 x 7-1/2	SCRAP

Cardstock*

A 12 x 4-1/2	I 4-1/2 x 4-1/2	H 6 x 3
	I 4-1/2 x 4-1/2	
	E 2 x 2	E 2 x 2	SCRAP

Cardstock*

C 4-1/2 x 6-1/2
K 2 x 2	K 2 x 2	K 2 x 2
		SCRAP

Cardstock

| F 2 x 2 |
| F 2 x 2 |
| L 2 x 2 |
| L 2 x 2 |
| L 2 x 2 |
| SCRAP |

Cardstock

| D 2 x 2 |
| D 2 x 2 |
| J 2 x 2 |
| J 2 x 2 |
| J 2 x 2 |
| J 2 x 2 |
| SCRAP |

© 2005 JRL PUBLICATIONS

*Identical papers

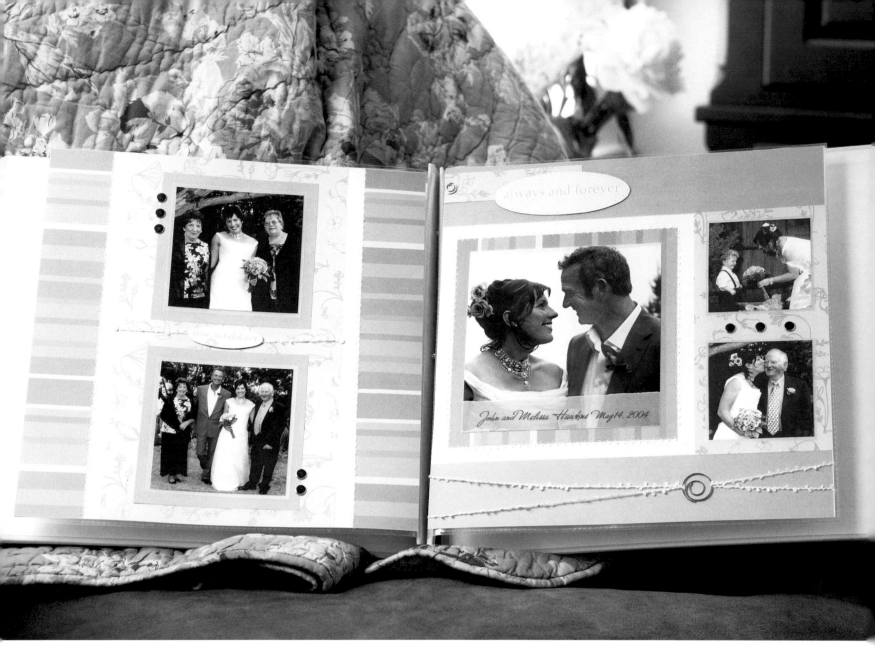

PUZZLE JUNKIE LIKE A DESIGNER PUZZLE, FIT THE NECESSARY PIECES TOGETHER

.... *Cutting Instructions* ....

B&T Paper

E 8 x 4
B 12 x 7
SCRAP

B&T Paper

A 12 x 2	A 12 x 2	F 7 x 7
		SCRAP

Cardstock

D 2 x 12	
D 2 x 12	
C 5 x 5	C 5 x 5
	SCRAP

© 2005 JRL PUBLICATIONS

Layout Materials

12" x 12" Base Cardstock (2)
12" x 12" Cardstock (1)
12" x 12" B&T Paper (2)

Left Page
Dimensions

A   12" x 2" (2)
B   12" x 7"
C   5" x 5" (2)

Right Page
Dimensions

D   2" x 12" (2)
E   8" x 4"
F   7" x 7"

Photo
Suggestions

1   4" x 4" (2)
2   6" x 6"
3   3" x 3" (2)

Suggested Title

1   1" x 4-1/2"

Suggested
Journaling

1   1" x 6"

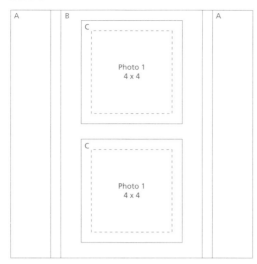

A | B | C

Photo 1
4 x 4

C

Photo 1
4 x 4

A

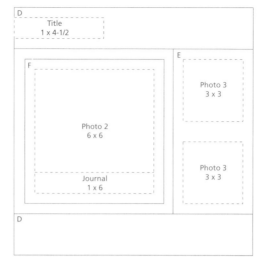

D

Title
1 x 4-1/2

F

E

Photo 3
3 x 3

Photo 2
6 x 6

Photo 3
3 x 3

Journal
1 x 6

D

1 Using one 12" x 12" cardstock as your base, attach one piece A to the left and right sides of the page, keeping the edges flush.

2 Attach piece B to the center of the page, placing it 1/2" from the inside edges of pieces A.

3 Attach pieces C to piece B, 1/2" from the top and bottom and 1" from the side edges.

4 Attach the specified photos (photos 1) to the appropriate area, centering it on the mat.

1 Using one 12" x 12" cardstock as your base, attach pieces D to the top and bottom of the page, keeping the edges flush.

2 Attach piece E to the right edge of the page between both pieces D, flush with the edges of pieces D.

3 Attach piece F centered between pieces D, keeping 1/2" from the edges.

4 Attach the specified photos (photos 2-3) to the appropriate areas, centering them on the mats.

Puzzle Junkie

Tip & Technique
Embossing

Journaling Idea
Journal on vellum and place it directly over the edge of your photo.

For full recipe and Tip & Technique see index pg. 127

© 2005 JRL PUBLICATIONS

Layout Materials

12" x 12" Base Cardstock (2)
12" x 12" Cardstock (2)
12" x 12" B&T Paper (3)

Left Page Dimensions

A 12" x 9"
B 9" x 7"
C 1-1/2" x 4-1/2"

Right Page Dimensions

D 4" x 4"
E 4" x 8"
F 1-1/2" x 12"
G 6-1/2" X 8"
H 4-1/2" x 6-1/2" (2)

Photo Suggestions

1 3" x 3" (3)
2 8" x 6"
3 4" x 6" (2)

Suggested Title

1 1" x 4"

Suggested Journaling

1 3-1/2" x 3-1/2"

LEFT

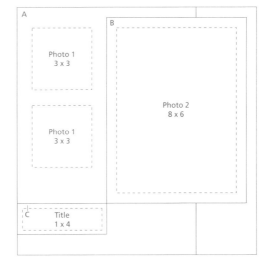

A

B

Photo 1
3 x 3

Photo 1
3 x 3

Photo 2
8 x 6

C Title
1 x 4

RIGHT

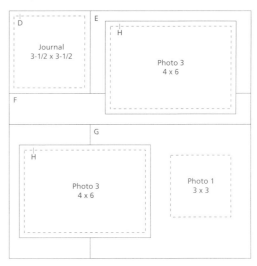

D Journal
3-1/2 x 3-1/2

E

H

Photo 3
4 x 6

F

G

H

Photo 3
4 x 6

Photo 1
3 x 3

LEFT

1 Using one 12" x 12" cardstock as your base, attach piece A to the top left side of the page, keeping the edges flush.

2 Attach piece B to the top of piece A, 1/2" from the right side and top of the page.

3 Attach piece C to piece A, 3/4" from the bottom of the page, keeping the left edge flush.

4 Attach the specified photos (photos 1-2) to the appropriate areas, centering them on the mats.

RIGHT

1 Using one 12" x 12" cardstock as your base, attach piece D to the top left corner of the page, keeping the edges flush.

2 Attach piece E to the top right corner of the page next to piece D, keeping the edges flush.

3 Attach piece F below pieces D and E, keeping the edges flush.

4 Attach piece G to the bottom right corner of the page, keeping the edges flush.

5 Attach one piece H to the top of pieces E and F, 1/2" from the top of the page and 3/4" from the right side of the page.

6 Attach remaining piece H to the bottom left corner of the page, 1/2" from the left side and 1" from the bottom of the page.

7 Attach the specified photos (photos 1 and 3) to the appropriate areas, centering them on the mats.

Tip & Technique
Dry embossing

Journaling Idea
Use descriptive words as title embellishments, adding them to various places on the page.

For full recipe and Tip & Technique see index pg. 128

© 2005 JRL PUBLICATIONS

WINNING LAYOUT GIVE YOUR MEMORIES THE ATTENTION THEY DESERVE WITH THIS WINNING LAYOUT

········· *Cutting Instructions* ·····························

B&T Paper*

A
12 x 9

SCRAP

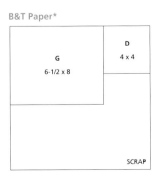

B&T Paper*

G
6-1/2 x 8

D
4 x 4

SCRAP

Cardstock**

B
9 x 7

SCRAP

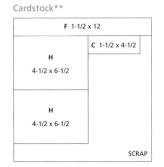

Cardstock**

F 1-1/2 x 12

C 1-1/2 x 4-1/2

H
4-1/2 x 6-1/2

H
4-1/2 x 6-1/2

SCRAP

B&T Paper

E
4 x 8

SCRAP

© 2005 JRL PUBLICATIONS

*Identical papers **Identical papers

TUB TIME

Mmmmmmmmmmmm this is Mom's FAVORITE time of day. You sit in the bubbles and wash all your cares away. You splash and giggle and soak until your little toes and fingers are as wrinkled as an elephant and then you laugh at the wrinkles. I get you out and wrap you in a warm towel and for the first time all day, you sit still and let me hold you. I drink in the delicious smell of your clean hair and I marvel, once again, that you are my baby girl.

SAGE

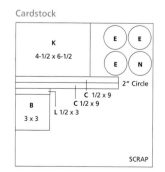

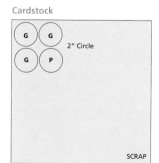

DYNAMIC DESIGN THIS DYNAMIC DESIGN EMPHASIZES A CLEAR CENTER OF INTEREST

Cutting Instructions

Cardstock

H 7-1/2 x 5-1/2	J 4-1/2 x 4-1/2	D
		D
	J 4-1/2 x 4-1/2	D
		D
		O
SCRAP		2" Circle

Cardstock

A 3 x 9	I 4-1/2 x 6-1/2	F
		F
		F
		M
SCRAP		2" Circle

Cardstock

K 4-1/2 x 6-1/2	E	E
	E	N
		2" Circle
C 1/2 x 9		
C 1/2 x 9		
B 3 x 3	L 1/2 x 3	
SCRAP		

Cardstock

G	G	
G	P	2" Circle
SCRAP		

© 2005 JRL PUBLICATIONS

Layout Materials

12" x 12" Base Cardstock (2)
12" x 12" Cardstock (4)

Left Page Dimensions

A 3" x 9"
B 3" x 3"
C 1/2" x 9" (2)
D 2" circle (4)
E 2" circle (3)
F 2" circle (3)
G 2" circle (3)
H 7-1/2" x 5-1/2"

Right Page Dimensions

I 4-1/2" x 6-1/2"
J 4-1/2" x 4-1/2" (2)
K 4-1/2" x 6-1/2"
L 1/2" x 3"
M 2" circle
N 2" circle
O 2" circle
P 2" circle

Photo Suggestions

1 7" x 5"
2 4" x 6" (2)
3 4" x 4" (2)

Suggested Title

1 1-1/2" x 5-1/2"

Suggested Journaling

1 7-1/2" x 2-3/4"

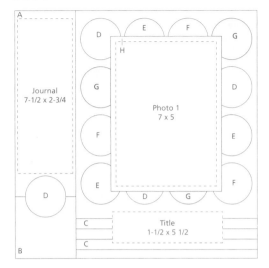

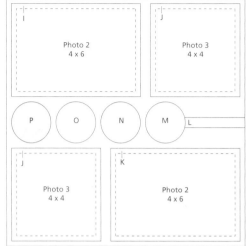

LEFT

1 Using one 12" x 12" cardstock as your base, attach piece A to the top left corner of the page, keeping the edges flush.

2 Attach piece B to the bottom left corner of the page, keeping the edges flush.

3 Attach the two piece C strips across the bottom of the page, placing them 1/2" from the bottom and 1/2" apart, keeping the side edges flush.

4 Arrange pieces D, E, F, and G circles on the page as shown and attach.

5 Attach piece H to the page, placing it 1" from the top and 2" from the right edge.

6 Attach the specified photo (photo 1) to the appropriate area, centering it on the mat.

RIGHT

1 Using one 12" x 12" cardstock as your base, attach one piece I to the upper left, placing it 1/4" from the left and top edges.

2 Attach one piece J to the upper right, placing it 1/4" from the right and top edges.

3 Attach the remaining piece J to the lower left, placing it 1/4" from the left and bottom edges.

4 Attach piece K to the lower right, placing it 1/4" from the right and bottom edges.

5 Attach piece L 5-1/2" from the bottom, keeping the right edges flush.

6 Arrange pieces M, N, O, and P circles on the page as shown and attach.

7 Attach the specified photos (photos 2-3) to the appropriate areas, centering them on the mats.

Dynamic Design

Tip & Technique
Coluzzle® templates

Journaling Idea
Add interest
by hanging
page titles from
dominant photos.

For full recipe and Tip & Technique see index pg. 128

© 2005 JRL PUBLICATIONS

Layout Materials

12" x 12" Base Cardstock (2)
12" x 12" Cardstock (2)
12" x 12" B&T Paper (3)

*Left Page
Dimensions*

A 12" x 2"
B 6" x 3"
C 6" x 7"
D 6" x 3"
E 6" x 7"

*Right Page
Dimensions*

F 6" x 3"
G 6" x 3"
H 6" x 6"
I 12" x 2"
J 12" x 4"

*Photo
Suggestions*

1 5" x 7"
2 3" x 3" (2)
3 5" x 5" (2)

Suggested Title

1 11" x 1-1/2"

*Suggested
Journaling*

1 1" x 4" (10)

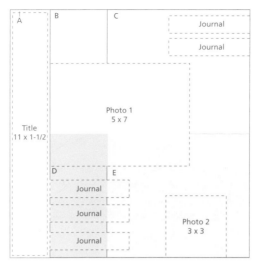

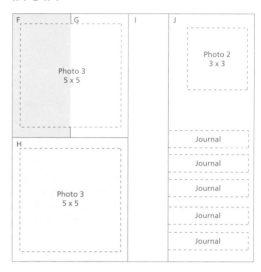

1 Using one 12" x 12" cardstock as your base, attach piece A to the left side of the page, keeping the edges flush.

2 Attach piece B to the right side of piece A, keeping the edges flush.

3 Attach piece C to the top right side of the page, keeping the edges flush.

4 Attach piece D to the bottom of the page below piece B and to the right of piece A, keeping the bottom edges flush.

5 Attach piece E to the bottom right corner of the page, keeping the edges flush.

6 Attach the specified photos (photos 1-2) to the appropriate areas.

1 Using one 12" x 12" cardstock as your base, attach piece F to the top left corner of the page, keeping the edges flush.

2 Attach piece G to the right of piece F, keeping the edges flush.

3 Attach piece H to the bottom left corner of the page under pieces F and G, keeping the edges flush.

4 Attach piece I to the right of pieces G and H, keeping the edges flush.

5 Attach piece J to the right side of the page, keeping the edges flush.

6 Attach the specified photos (photos 2-3) to the appropriate areas.

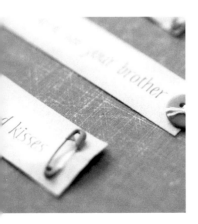

Tip & Technique
**Anchor journaling
with accents**

Journaling Idea
**Apply your
journaling
boxes at slightly
different angles to
add visual interest.**

*For full recipe and Tip &
Technique see index pg. 128*

© 2005 JRL PUBLICATIONS

GIVE ME TEN JOURNAL THE TOP TEN REASONS WHY, WITH PHOTOS TO TELL YOUR STORY

········· *Cutting Instructions* ···

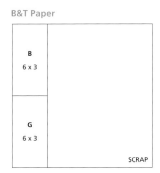
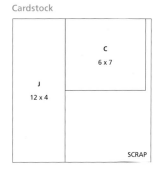
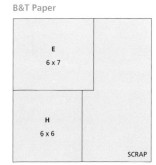
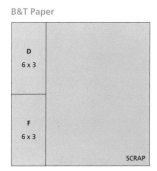

Cardstock	B&T Paper	Cardstock	B&T Paper	B&T Paper
A 12 x 2 / **I** 12 x 2	**B** 6 x 3 / **G** 6 x 3 / SCRAP	**C** 6 x 7 / **J** 12 x 4 / SCRAP	**E** 6 x 7 / **H** 6 x 6 / SCRAP	**D** 6 x 3 / **F** 6 x 3 / SCRAP

© 2005 JRL PUBLICATIONS

JULY LAYOUT (page 8)

Recipe

Birthday Bash Paper Packet
Cranberry Cardstock
Star Spangled Blue Cardstock
Dimensional Elements Classic Alphabet
Dimensional Elements Slide Frames
Dimensional Elements Bookplates
My Accents™ White
My Accents™ Cranberry
White Daisy Eyelets
Sandpaper

SOLDIER LAYOUT (page 8)

Recipe

My Acrylix™ Stamp Set, Air Mail
Vintage Travel Paper Packet
Vintage Travel My Stickease™ Assortment
My Accents™ Pewter
Bamboo Exclusive Inks™ Pad
Cocoa Exclusive Inks™ Pad
Pewter Eyelets
Natural Hemp

MY SON LAYOUT (page 8)

Recipe

Rowdy Paper Packet
White Daisy Cardstock
Dimensional Elements Bookplates
Autumn Harvest Sassy Strands™
Hinges
My Accents™ Outdoor Denim
My Accents™ Garden Green
Silver Eyelets

ELEGANT CONTEXT (page 16)

Tip & Technique - Chalking

Soft chalks are an excellent way to add more color to your paper or an image, yet keep the soft, warm look you want. Using a cotton-tip swab or chalk applicator, add a little drama to your photo mats by chalking them a little darker than the paper.

Recipe

Heaven Sent Paper Packet
Heaven Sent My Stickease™ Assortment
White Daisy Organdy Ribbon
My Accents™ Buttercup
My Accents™ Heavenly Blue
Seafoam Eyelets
Heavenly Blue Eyelets
Buttercup Eyelets
Spring Soft Chalks
Vellum

ASYMMETRIC (page 18)

Tip & Technique - Antiquing Paper

For a touch of elegance and authenticity, antique your papers by dabbing the bristles of an inked stipple brush onto the edges of your paper. Inks in browns and tans work especially well for this technique.

Recipe

Elegant Bouquet Paper Packet
Desert Sand Exclusive Inks™ Pad
Ivory Organdy Ribbon
My Accents™ Pewter
Pewter Eyelets
Sponge Daubers
Needle and Thread

SILVER SCREEN (page 20)

Tip & Technique - Crinkled Vellum

Add a speckled look to background papers by dabbing ink on them with crinkled vellum. Crinkle vellum into a ball, press it onto a stamp pad, then lightly "stamp" your paper with the vellum.

Recipe

My Acrylix™ Stamp Set, Designed for You
On Your Toes Paper Packet
Buttercup Cardstock
Baby Pink Cardstock
Baby Pink Exclusive Inks™ Pad
Vellum
White Grosgrain Ribbon
Paper Circle Tags
My Accents™ White
White Eyelets

FILLING SPACES (page 22)

Tip & Technique - Making Paper Look like Leather

For a rugged, natural impression, make your scrapbook paper look like leather!

Step 1: Spray your paper with water using a spray bottle. Get it quite wet.

Step 2: Scrunch your wet paper into a small ball. (Some tearing may occur which will add to the rustic look of the paper.)

Step 3: Carefully smooth out paper.

Step 4: Iron the paper flat using medium heat and no steam.

Step 5: When completely dry, use a round sponge and ink to darken the paper.

Recipe

Giddy Up Paper Packet
Chocolate Cardstock
Desert Sand Cardstock
Solid Metallic Cardstock Combo
Chocolate Exclusive Inks™ Pad
Tan Hemp
Paper Circle Tags
My Accents™ Gold
Silver Eyelets
3-D Foam Squares
Stipple Brush

© 2005 JRL PUBLICATIONS

MIXING ELEMENTS (page 24)

Tip & Technique - Chalk Popping

Create vibrant stamped images that really pop. Stamp a solid image and while the ink is still damp, use a cotton-tip swab or chalk applicator to apply soft chalk in a slightly darker color.

Recipe

My Acrylix™ Stamp Set, Frightenin' Fun
At the Game Paper Packet
Outdoor Denim Cardstock
Cranberry Cardstock
Colonial White Cardstock
Outdoor Denim Background & Texture Paper
Autumn Terracotta Exclusive Inks™ Pad
Decorative Wire
Empressor® Guide
Embossing Stylus Medium
Tan Hemp
Autumn Soft Chalks

COLUMN COMPOSITION (page 26)

Tip & Technique - Highlight Journaling with Chalk

Highlight specific journaling words by cutting out a rectangular cardstock frame that fits around your chosen word. Place the frame around the word, choose a soft chalk that coordinates with your layout, then use a cotton-tip swab or chalk applicator to brush over the top of the word.

Recipe

My Acrylix™ Stamp Set, Best Friends
My Reflections Collection™ Best Friends Kit
Vineyard Berry Exclusive Inks™ Pad
Ocean Exclusive Inks™ Pad
Hinges
Summer Soft Chalks

SIMPLE CONTRAST (page 28)

Tip & Technique - Liquid Appliqué™

Liquid Appliqué can make stamped images look incredibly realistic. Use it for snow, ice cream, feathers, popcorn, and practically anything that needs texture.

Step 1: Apply Liquid Appliqué onto a stamped image in dabs, dots, stripes, or swirls.

Step 2: Using a heat tool, heat the image until puffy.

Step 3: (Optional) To color the white liquid, add a drop or two of re-inker to the liquid before heating, or try chalking it after it has been heated and dries.

Recipe

My Acrylix™ Stamp Set, Believe Caps
Traditional Holiday Paper Packet
Traditional Holiday My Stickease™ Assortment
Chocolate Exclusive Inks™ Pad
Round Sponge
My Accents™ Pewter
Scrapbook Kids Outfits-1
White Liquid Appliqué™

COLOR CELEBRATION (page 30)

Tip & Technique - Dimensional Elements

For bold accents or titles, use Dimensional Elements which are die-cuts made of thick, sturdy material that can be decorated with stamps, paper, chalks, markers, and more. Apply Liquid Glass with a paintbrush for a shiny, lacquer finish.

Recipe

My Acrylix™ Stamp Set, Best Friends
My Acrylix™ Stamp Set, Girly Girl
Stylin' Paper Packet
Stylin' My Stickease™ Assortment
Black Exclusive Inks™ Pad
Dimensional Elements Bookplates
Dimensional Elements Classic Alphabet
My Accents™ White Daisy
My Accents™ Black
My Accents™ Pink
Black Grosgrain Ribbon
Liquid Glass
Corner Rounder

AESTHETIC BALANCE (page 32)

Tip & Technique - Using Marker Ink on Stamps

To add colorful variety to a solid stamp image, color the stamp with different markers instead of inking with one stamp pad. A quick puff of warm breath will re-moisten the ink before stamping.

Recipe

My Acrylix™ Stamp Set, School Fun
Garden Green Background & Texture Paper
Golden Ember Cardstock
Colonial White Cardstock
Barn Red Cardstock
Garden Green Cardstock
Bamboo Exclusive Inks™ Pad
Autumn Harvest Exclusive Inks™ Marker Set
My Accents™ Garden Green
My Accents™ Colonial White
Dimensional Elements Bookplates
Stipple Brush

VISUAL TEXTURE (page 34)

Tip & Technique - Add Dimension with 3-D Foam Squares

For visual interest, add depth to your pages by mounting small images, titles, or photos on 3-D foam squares. They literally pop out from the page!

Recipe

My Acrylix™ Stamp Set, Vroom Caps
Rustic Trails Paper Packet
Rustic Trails My Stickease™ Assortment
Cocoa Exclusive Inks™ Pad
Bamboo Exclusive Inks™ Pad
Natural Hemp
Garden Green My Accents™ Accessories
Pewter My Accents™ Accessories
Photo Hangers
Vellum
Coluzzle® Hula Uppercase
Coluzzle® Swivel Knife
Coluzzle® Cutting Mat
3D Foam Squares

© 2005 JRL PUBLICATIONS

CREATIVE RHYTHM (page 36)

*Tip & Technique - Tinting Black &
White Photos with Ink*

Add classy highlights to black & white photos
by lightly shading select areas with ink from a
stamp pad. While the ink is wet, blend it with
a blending pen. Continue to add layers of ink
and blend until you have the desired color.

Recipe

Between Friends Paper Packet
Between Friends Level 1 Kit
Desert Sand Exclusive Inks™ Pad
Pink Carnation Exclusive Inks™ Pad
Blush Eyelets
Paper Circle Tags
Vellum
White Daisy Organdy Ribbon
My Accents™ Pewter
Blending Pen

HARMONY (page 38)

Tip & Technique - Accenting with Hemp

One of the easiest ways to add rustic appeal
is by accenting with hemp. Use it to anchor
embellishments, hang tags, or as a decorative
element all its own.

Recipe

My Acrylix™ Stamp Set, Giddy Up Alphabet
Giddy Up Paper Packet
Chocolate Cardstock
Desert Sand Exclusive Inks™ Pad
My Accents™ Pewter
Pewter Eyelets
3-D Foam Squares
Tan Hemp
Paper Circle Tags

ECHOES (page 40)

*Tip & Technique - Using Photos
with a Letter Template*

Wondering what to do with those extra photos
and photo scraps? Alphabet templates are the
perfect solution. Simply lay the template over
the photo, trace your letters, and cut out. It's
a fun, coordinating look for photos of water,
sand, fall leaves, and more!

Recipe

Beach House Paper Packet
Beach House My Stickease™ Assortment
My Accents™ Pewter
Vellum
Tan Hemp
Block Shadow Alphabet Stencil

ADD AN ELEMENT (page 42)

Tip & Technique - Sewing

Stitching adds a homespun feel to your layouts.
For evenly spaced stitches, make uniform holes
in your paper with a piercing tool or large
needle before hand stitching. Don't forget
the sewing machine for zigzag and
straight stitching.

Recipe

My Acrylix™ Stamp Set, Vroom Caps
My Acrylix™ Stamp Set, Girly Girl
My Acrylix™ Stamp Set, Alphabet Solos™ S
My Acrylix™ Stamp Set, Alphabet Solos™ I
Hollyhock Exclusive Inks™ Pad
Photo Clips
White Daisy My Accents™ Accessories
Colonial White Waxy Flax
Dimensional Elements Bookplates
White Paint
Stitching

KEPT IN PROPORTION (page 44)

Tip & Technique - Paper Rolling

Highlight a favorite scrapbook photo by using
the paper rolling technique on the photo mat.

Step 1: Attach your photo to cardstock and
tear around the photo, leaving a 1/2" to 1"
mat. Tear the cardstock so that the white torn
edge can be seen behind the photo.

Step 2: Curl the mat edges forward around a
large nail, wooden skewer, or any other object
that is long and skinny.

Step 3: For an even more rustic look, dab a bit
of brown ink on the torn white edges using a
round sponge.

Recipe

My Acrylix™ Stamp Set, Heritage
My Reflections Collection™ Pride kit
White Daisy Cardstock
My Accents™ Cranberry
Tan Hemp
Cranberry Grosgrain Ribbon
Silver Brads
Silver Eyelets
Cranberry Embossing Powder
White Embossing Powder

PHOTO SHAPES (page 46)

*Tip & Technique - Making Buckles
out of Paper Tags*

Buckles are unique embellishments that are
easy to make using paper tags. Simply remove
the paper center of the tag, and then fold
strips of paper around opposite sides of the
metal tag frame. Customize the "belt" using
eyelets or brads.

Recipe

My Acrylix™ Stamp Set, All You Need
Indian Corn Blue Cardstock
Barn Red Cardstock
Goldrush Cardstock
Olive Cardstock
White Daisy Cardstock
Indian Corn Blue Exclusive Inks™ Pad
Barn Red Exclusive Inks™ Pad
Goldrush Exclusive Inks™ Pad
Olive Exclusive Inks™ Pad
Block Shadow Alphabet Stencil
My Accents™ Pewter
Paper Square Tags

BEAUTY IN REPETITION (page 48)

Tip & Technique - Printing on Vellum

Creative sentiments become graceful art when
printed on vellum. Simply type your text on a
computer and then run vellum through your
printer as if it were regular printer paper. Lay
the vellum sheet over your project and mark
it for cutting.

© 2005 JRL PUBLICATIONS

Recipe

My Acrylix™ Stamp Set, Childhood Boy
Pawsitively Pals Paper Packet
Dutch Blue Exclusive Inks™ Pad
Garden Green Exclusive Inks™ Pad
Dimensional Elements Bookplates
Colonial White My Accents™ Accessories
Garden Green My Accents™ Accessories
Colonial White Waxy Flax
Vellum

DREAMY LOOK (page 52)

Tip & Technique - Covering Buttons

Personalize your button accents with coordinating patterned paper. Use sticky dots to attach the paper to the button and the button to your page.

Recipe

My Reflections Collection™ Graduation Kit
Vintage Travel Paper Packet
Vintage Travel My Stickease™ Assortment
Black Organdy Ribbon
Black Grosgrain Ribbon
Photo Hangers
Photo Clips
Pewter My Accents™ Accessories
Dimensional Elements Basic Shapes
Paper Circle Tags

INTERESTING VARIATION (page 54)

Tip & Technique - Empressor® Guide

Create your own patterned paper in stripes, checks, and plaids using a grid-marked Empressor Guide and an Empressing Tool.

Step 1: Lay your paper face down on the Empressor Guide.

Step 2: Using the grid lines for accuracy, align your paper so it hangs off the right edge of the guide.

Step 3: Trace the right edge of the guide with the Empressor® Tool, creating a raised line in your paper.

Step 4: Repeat the process for the desired stripe or checkered look.

Step 5: (Optional) Turn the paper over and sand the raised lines.

Recipe

My Acrylix™ Stamp Set, Brushstroke Garden
Plum Mist Cardstock
Smokey Plum Cardstock
Bamboo Cardstock
Olive Cardstock
Olive Exclusive Inks™ Pad
Plum Mist Exclusive Inks™ Pad
Smokey Plum Exclusive Inks™ Pad
Dimensional Elements Bookplates
My Accents™ Garden Green
Vanilla Cream Waxy Flax
Vellum
Olive Eyelets
Empressor® Tool
Empressor® Guide
Sandpaper

ELEGANT SHOWCASE (page 56)

Tip & Technique - Printing on My Stickease™ Artwork

Creative journaling on My Stickease™ art draws the eye to your heartfelt sentiments.

Step 1: Print your journaling on standard printer paper.

Step 2: Hold the paper up to a light source such as a light box, window, or even the computer screen.

Step 3: Attach My Stickease™ art on the top of the printed text. You should be able to see through it because of the light source behind it.

Step 4: Run the paper through your printer once again. The text will print right on top of the image!

Step 5: Cut out the image and attach to your scrapbook page.

Recipe

My Acrylix™ Stamp Set, Air Mail
My Acrylix™ Stamp Set, Love Tags
Vintage Travel Paper Packet
Vintage Travel My Stickease™ Assortment
Chocolate Exclusive Inks™ Pad
My Accents™ Pewter
Coluzzle® Circle
Coluzzle® Tags
Black Gingham Ribbon

Ivory Organdy Ribbon
Black Waxy Flax
Vellum
Paper Circle Tags
Black Embossing Powder
3-D Foam Squares

A NEW PERSPECTIVE (page 58)

Tip & Technique - Dividing a Large Photo Designation into Several Smaller Areas

An easy way to add more photos to a page while preserving the design concept is to transform a large photo area into four smaller photo spaces. Leave a bit of mat space around each small photo to set them off.

Recipe

My Acrylix™ Stamp Set, The Simple Things
Flower Power Paper Packet
Flower Power My Stickease™ Assortment
Sweet Leaf Exclusive Inks™ Pad
My Accents™ Buttercup
Paper Circle Tags

GRAPHIC TEXTURE (page 60)

Tip & Technique - Direct-to-Paper Ink

For a random splash of fun, use your ink pad like a paintbrush, running it right over the top of your paper wherever you'd like ink to appear. Ink as much as you want with as many colors as you want.

Recipe

My Acrylix™ Stamp Set, Believe Caps
My Acrylix™ Stamp Set, Believe Lowercase
My Acrylix™ Stamp Set, Amoré Lowercase
My Acrylix™ Stamp Set, Love Tags
Antique Lace Paper Packet
Bamboo Cardstock
Outdoor Denim Cardstock
Barn Red Cardstock
White Daisy Cardstock
My Accents™ Pewter
Colonial White Waxy Flax

© 2005 JRL PUBLICATIONS

CONTRASTING ELEMENTS (page 62)

Tip & Technique - Using Photos as Background & Texture Paper

For a fun look, enlarge one of your photos to 8" x 10" and then use it just as you would Background & Texture paper!

Recipe

My Acrylix™ Stamp Set, Believe Caps
My Acrylix™ Stamp Set, You and Me
Cranberry Cardstock
Dutch Blue Cardstock
Cranberry Background & Texture Paper
Cranberry Exclusive Inks™ Pad
Tan Hemp
My Accents™ Cranberry

DUPLICATE PATTERNS (page 64)

Tip & Technique - Make Empty Spots Pop

Look for ways to make empty space part of your layout's theme. Use a frame stamp and stamp a simple decoration in an empty square, or use an image that complements your theme and create spaces that support your layout.

Recipe

My Acrylix™ Stamp Set, Girly Girls
Lovely Leaves My Stickease™ Assortment
Lovely Leaves Paper Packet
Ponderosa Pine Cardstock
Sweet Leaf Cardstock
Sweet Leaf Background & Texture Paper
Ponderosa Pine Exclusive Inks™ Pad
Sweet Leaf Exclusive Inks™ Pad
My Accents™ White
Ponderosa Pine Waxy Flax

ABSTRACT (page 66)

Tip & Technique - Fill with Embellishments

If you love a particular scrapbook page design but your photo is a bit small, simply attach your photo, and then fill the space with embellishments. Make the concept your own!

Recipe

Rustic Trail Paper Packet
Rustic Trail My Stickease™ Assortment
Cocoa Exclusive Inks™ Pad
Dutch Blue Grosgrain Ribbon
Pewter My Accents™ Accessories
Hinges
Photo Clips
Sandpaper
Stitching

UNIFIED WHOLE (page 68)

Tip & Technique - Accenting with Ribbon

Color-coordinating ribbons add bright 3-D flair to layouts. When used as a photo border, ribbons can "anchor" your picture and draw attention to your focal point.

Recipe

My Acrylix™ Stamp Set, Whimsy Caps
White Daisy Cardstock
Cranberry Cardstock
Black Cardstock
Sunny Yellow Cardstock
Cranberry Grosgrain Ribbon
Sunkiss Yellow Grosgrain Ribbon
Black Gingham Ribbon
My Accents™ Black
My Accents™ Cranberry
Cranberry Waxy Flax
Paper Circle Tags
Heating Tool
Embossing Set
1/8" Ribbon: black, pink, black polka-dot

DESIGNER'S EYE (page 70)

Tip & Technique - Watercolor

For a soft, sophisticated look, watercolor your stamped images. Using a waterbrush makes what looks like an advanced technique quite easy!

Step 1: Stamp your chosen image on paper. If using a line image, stamp with permanent black ink.

Step 2: Make your "artist's palette" by putting a drop of re-inker in the open lid of the coordinating ink pad or, with the ink pad closed, squeeze the lid so it touches the pad and picks up ink, then open the lid.

Step 3: Squeeze a bit of water into the tip of your waterbrush (more water will give you lighter colors and less water will give you darker colors).

Step 4: Dip your brush into the ink and paint your stamped image. We recommend you practice on scrap paper first. Hint: Determine where the light source is coming from, leave the side closest to the light a lighter color, and shade the areas away from the light source much darker (on solid stamped images, a small area is often left white where the light source is located).

Step 5: For a light, neutral background, use a lot of water and a brown or tan re-inker and shade the area around the stamped image.

Step 6: Allow image to dry completely.

Recipe

My Acrylix™ Stamp Set, Paradise
My Acrylix™ Stamp Set, Hang 10
Laid Back Paper Packet
Orange Exclusive Inks™ Pad
Olive Exclusive Inks™ Pad
Vineyard Berry Exclusive Inks™ Pad
Sunflower Exclusive Inks™ Pad
Dutch Blue Exclusive Inks™ Pad
Chocolate Exclusive Inks™ Marker
Sunflower Exclusive Inks™ Marker
Olive Exclusive Inks™ Marker
Vineyard Berry Exclusive Inks™ Marker
White Daisy My Accents™ Accessories
Dimensional Elements Bookplates
Photo Hangers
Colonial White Waxy Flax
Hinges
Medium Waterbrush

© 2005 JRL PUBLICATIONS

SIMPLE PLEASURES (page 72)

Tip & Technique - Softening Edges

To soften the edge of cardstock mats in an elegant layout, use a sharp, open scissors blade and lightly scrape along the edge of the cardstock, revealing the white inner core. To add a distressed effect, add ink to your now softened edges.

Recipe

My Acrylix™ Stamp Set, Heritage Caps
My Acrylix™ Stamp Set, Memories
Heirloom Paper Packet
Heirloom My Stickease™ Assortment
Desert Sand Exclusive Inks™ Pad
Pewter My Accents™ Accessories
Dimensional Elements Bookplates
Hinges
Photo Hangers
Photo Clips
Sponge Daubers
Round Sponge

FAB FIFTEEN (page 74)

Tip & Technique - Stamping on Ribbon

Pretty ribbons become more than page accents when you use them for journaling!

Step 1: Print your journaling on standard printer paper.

Step 2: Hold the paper up to a light source such as a light box, window, or even the computer screen.

Step 3: Using temporary adhesive, attach your ribbon over the top of the printed text. You should be able to see through it because of the light source behind it.

Step 4: Run the paper through your printer once again. The text will print right on top of the ribbon!

Step 5: Remove the ribbon from the paper and attach to your layout.

Recipe

Nature's Treasures Paper Packet
Nature's Treasures My Stickease™ Assortment
Chocolate Exclusive Inks™ Pad
Vellum

Autumn Leaves Brass Stencil
My Accents™ Pewter

PORTRAIT COLLECTION (page 76)

Tip & Technique - Foil

Foil paper is elegant and surprisingly easy to work with. You can emboss it, mold it, cut it, and even paint on it! These shapes were cut out, painted with white acrylic paint, and after dry, were sanded to let the foil shine through.

Recipe

My Acrylix™ Stamp Set, Alphabet Solos™ S
My Acrylix™ Stamp Set, Alphabet Solos™ U
My Acrylix™ Stamp Set, Alphabet Solos™ M
My Acrylix™ Stamp Set, Alphabet Solos™ E
My Acrylix™ Stamp Set, Alphabet Solos™ R
My Acrylix™ Stamp Set, Alphabet Solos™ F
My Acrylix™ Stamp Set, Alphabet Solos™ N
My Acrylix™ Stamp Set, Sans Small Uppercase
Building Blocks Paper Packet
Moonstruck Exclusive Inks™ Pad
Vellum
White Daisy My Accents™ Accessories
Silver My Accents™ Accessories
Cranberry My Accents™ Accessories
Silver Foil Sheets
Cranberry Eyelets
White Daisy Grosgrain Ribbon
Cranberry Waxy Flax
Round Sponge
Stitching
White Paint

ACCENT EMPHASIS (page 78)

Tip & Technique - The All-in-One My Reflections Collection™ Kits

My Reflections Collection™ Kits are the perfect, all-in-one solution for easy scrapbooking. You can create two beautifully embellished pages using only the supplies in the kit. An instruction brochure is included or use your imagination!

Recipe

My Reflections Collection™ Happy Halloween Kit
Sunny Yellow Cardstock
Black Cardstock

Black Waxy Flax
Vellum

GOLDEN SECTION (page 80)

Tip & Technique - Circle Punches

Circle punches are amazing little tools that allow you to easily cut circular shapes and embellishments. You can dress up an entire layout using a few complementary papers and a couple of circle punches.

Recipe

My Acrylix™ Stamp Set, Storytime Numbers
My Acrylix™ Stamp Set, In Stitches Lowercase
Cranberry Cardstock
Sunny Yellow Cardstock
White Daisy Cardstock
Black Cardstock
Cranberry Fleurs des Jardins™ Papers
Black Gingham Ribbon
Block Shadow Alphabet Stencil
Paper Rectangle Tags
Circle Punches - Various Sizes

DRAMATIC FASHION (page 82)

Tip & Technique - Combining Accents

Many accents can be used together to create a truly unique look. Use a large concho, a small concho, and a brad all nested together for a novel effect. Use your imagination with eyelets, buttons, and hinges, too!

Recipe

Independence Paper Packet
Independence My Stickease™ Assortment
Barn Red Cardstock
Bamboo Exclusive Inks™ Pad
My Accents™ Outdoor Denim
Sandpaper

FORM & FUNCTION (page 84)

Tip & Technique - Cracked Glass

The cracked-glass technique gives the impression you are seeing your artwork through the time-worn cracks of a beautiful antique window.

© 2005 JRL PUBLICATIONS

Step 1: Gather the following materials: Clear embossing powder, a clear double-sided adhesive sheet, a craft heater, scratch paper, tweezers, scissors, and your artwork.

Step 2: Create your desired image, leaving a large margin around the image for trimming later. Your finished tones will be muted when seen through the cracked glass, so you may want to darken them a bit.

Step 3: Attach the clear adhesive sheet, trimmed with large margins to fit your image, to the front of your artwork. Peel the backing off the adhesive sheet so you can see your artwork through it and have a sticky surface.

Step 4: Pour a generous amount of clear embossing powder evenly on a piece of scratch paper covering a large enough area to encompass your image. Place your artwork, sticky-side down, on the powder. Press evenly.

Step 5: Lift art off powder and heat-emboss. Immediately after heat-embossing, repeat this procedure eight times. Do not allow your project to cool between embossings. Handle your artwork with tweezers as it will be very warm.

Step 6: After applying all the layers of embossing, allow your project to cool completely. Place in refrigerator or freezer if desired.

Step 7: Bend the artwork and watch the layers of embossing crack! Crack it as much as desired and in different directions.

Step 8: Trim your image to its desired size and attach with glue dots or another strong adhesive.

Recipe

My Acrylix™ Stamp Set, Goal!
Rowdy Paper Packet
Rowdy My Stickease™ Assortment
Outdoor Denim Exclusive Inks™ Pad
Black Exclusive Inks™ Pad
Zoom Alpha Series
My Accents™ Outdoor Denim
Adhesive Sheets
Embossing Set
Craft Heater

RISE TO THE OCCASION (page 88)

Tip & Technique - Paper Tearing

One of the simplest texture techniques is paper tearing. Using paper with a white core, tear down one side to the size you desire, exposing the white edge. If desired, add distressing to the edge with a sponge and tan or brown ink.

Recipe

My Acrylix™ Stamp Set, Fall
Harvest Paper Packet
Harvest My Stickease™ Assortment
Black Exclusive Inks™ Pad
My Accents™ Autumn Terracotta
My Accents™ Gold
Buttercup Organdy Ribbon

SCENIC BYWAY (page 90)

Tip & Technique - Fun Flock

Fun Flock adds fluffy, 3-D fun to any scrapbook page. Simply apply Liquid Appliqué to your layout, sprinkle Fun Flock over it, shake off excess powder, then set with a craft heater.

Recipe

Tropicana Level 1 Kit
Tropicana Paper Packet
Ocean Cardstock
Breeze Cardstock
Desert Sand Cardstock
My Accents™ White
White Fun Flock
Liquid Appliqué
Block Shadow Alphabet Stencil

HARMONIOUS PATTERNS (page 92)

Tip & Technique - Sanding Buttons

Give your button embellishments a time-worn look by sanding them with sandpaper.

Recipe

My Acrylix™ Stamp Set, Bubble Caps
My Acrylix™ Stamp Set, Let's Play Ball
Groovy Blossoms Paper Packet
Bamboo Cardstock
Sweet Leaf Exclusive Inks™ Pad

Cocoa Exclusive Inks™ Pad
Hollyhock Exclusive Inks™ Pad
Photo Clips
White Daisy My Accents™ Accessories
Garden Green My Accents™ Accessories
Hollyhock Eyelets
Olive Waxy Flax
Dimensional Elements Basic Shapes
Dimensional Elements Bookplates
Liquid Glass
Vellum

PLEASING PARADIGM (page 94)

Tip & Technique - Staples

Turn household items into eye-catching embellishments by using silver or colored staples to accent pages and tie layouts together.

Recipe

Great Outdoors Paper Packet
Great Outdoors My Stickease™ Assortment
My Legacy Writer® Black set
Colored Staples
Sandpaper

PHOTO FUSION (page 96)

Tip & Technique - Paper Piecing

For variety, create a stamp image using colored paper instead of ink.

Step 1: Determine the various colors you'll need for your stamp image.

Step 2: Stamp your image once on each of your chosen cardstock colors.

Step 3: Using Micro-tip Scissors, cut out the different parts of your stamp image from the appropriate colors of paper, i.e., green fish body, white gills, blue eye, black eyeball.

Step 4: Glue the image together, layer by layer, using the different color pieces.

Step 5: Attach to project.

Recipe

My Acrylix™ Stamp Set, Kissy Fish
Moonstruck Cardstock
Orange Cardstock

© 2005 JRL PUBLICATIONS

Cranberry Cardstock
Topiary Cardstock
Moonstruck Background & Texture Paper
Orange Background & Texture Paper
Topiary Background & Texture Paper
White Daisy Eyelets
My Accents™ White
Block Shadow Alphabet Stencil

GALLERY COLLECTION (page 98)

Tip & Technique - Rotate Concept to Complement Photos

If the subjects in your photo are facing the wrong way for your chosen scrapbook layout, don't be afraid to rotate the page concept. Each page design can be used as shown or can be rotated one turn to the right or left and even turned 180° for maximum versatility.

Recipe

My Acrylix™ Stamp Set, Beauty Seen
Great Outdoors Paper Packet
Great Outdoor My Stickease™ Assortment
White Daisy Cardstock
White Hemp
My Accents™ Pewter
Pewter Eyelets
Vellum

THEN & NOW (page 100)

Tip & Technique - Sassy Strands™

Soft Sassy Strands™ fibers add flair and dimension to your layouts. String them across page elements, create pretty bows, hang other accents from them, or wrap them around cards and tie closed.

Recipe

Precious Paisleys Paper Packet
Precious Paisleys My Stickease™ Assortment
Baby Pink Cardstock
Baby Pink Exclusive Inks™ Pad
White Daisy Exclusive Inks™ Re-Inker
Baby Pink My Accents™ Accessories
3/8" White Daisy Organdy Ribbon
5/8" White Daisy Organdy Ribbon

Sassy Strands™ Spring Harmony Collection
Paper Circle Tags
Photo Hangers
Colored Staples

CLEAR DIMENSION (page 102)

Tip & Technique - Liquid Glass

Finish off your tag art in style by applying Liquid Glass over the top for a glossy, shimmering look.

Recipe

My Acrylix™ Stamp Set, Beetle Bugs
My Acrylix™ Stamp Set, Precious Alphabet
My Acrylix™ Stamp Set, Girly Girl
My Acrylix™ Stamp Set, Life Is
Groovy Blossom Paper Packet
Groovy Blossom My Stickease™ Assortment
Hollyhock Exclusive Inks™ Pad
Cocoa Exclusive Inks™ Pad
Liquid Glass
White Daisy Grosgrain Ribbon
Dimensional Elements Classic Alphabet
Photo Hangers
White Paint

BALANCED BLOCKS (page 104)

Tip & Technique - Paper Crinkling

To easily add texture and dimension to your scrapbook page, after stamping your desired image on paper, crinkle up the stamped paper, smooth it out a bit, trim it, and attach the crinkled image to your layout.

Recipe

My Acrylix™ Stamp Set, Believe Lowercase
My Acrylix™ Stamp Set, Groovy
Buttercup Cardstock
Baby Pink Cardstock
Buttercup Background & Texture Paper
Baby Pink Background & Texture Paper
Vellum
Decorative Wire
Silver Brads
My Accents™ Pewter

My Accents™ Buttercup
White Daisy Organdy Ribbon
Spring Soft Chalks
Winter Soft Chalks
Paper Circle Tags
Paper Square Tags
Scrapbook Kids Costume Fun

EASY INSPIRATION (page 106)

Tip & Technique - Accenting Photos with My Stickease™

Use My Stickease™ artwork as creative corner accents for your photos. They are subtle, color-coordinated, and draw the eye to your treasured memory.

Recipe

Elegant Bouquet Paper Packet
Elegant Bouquet My Stickease™ Assortment
My Accents™ Cranberry

RISE 'N SHINE (page 108)

Tip & Technique - Clay Tiles

Personalized clay tiles are simple to create and make a bold statement on your layouts.

Step 1: Roll out the clay with a rolling pin to the desired thickness.

Step 2: Using a cutting tool and ruler, cut the clay to the desired shape.

Step 3: Stamp the clay tile with your inked stamp. Let dry.

Step 4: (Optional) Stamp your clay tile after it has dried completely.

Step 5: Attach with Liquid Glass or other strong adhesive.

Recipe

My Acrylix™ Stamp Set, Spring Leaves
Lovely Leaves Paper Packet
Olive Exclusive Inks™ Pad
Vellum
My Accents™ Pewter
Olive Waxy Flax
Sculpting Foam™

© 2005 JRL PUBLICATIONS

Stipple Brush
Liquid Glass
Staples

TREASURE TAGS (page 110)

Tip & Technique - Sponged Background

Create your own background paper by sponging ink onto cardstock. Experiment using different colors and different tones of the same color for a soft, artistic look.

Recipe

My Acrylix™ Stamp Set, Season of Change
Autumn Terracotta Cardstock
Goldrush Cardstock
Cranberry Cardstock
New England Ivy Cardstock
New England Ivy Exclusive Inks™ Pad
Autumn Terracotta Exclusive Inks™ Pad
Goldrush Exclusive Inks™ Pad
Cranberry Exclusive Inks™ Pad
My Accents™ Pewter
Pewter Eyelets
Natural Hemp
Round Sponge

PUZZLE JUNKIE (page 112)

Tip & Technique - Embossing

For that extra touch of shiny sophistication, try embossing your stamped images and sentiments!

Step 1: Ink your stamp with a tinted embossing ink pad. Stamp your image where desired.

Step 2: While the embossing ink is still wet, sprinkle it with your chosen color of embossing powder. Pour off the excess powder.

Step 3: Heat the image with a craft heater until set.

Recipe

My Acrylix™ Stamp Set, Wedding
Stylin' Paper Packet
Vellum
Sassy Strands™ White Daisy
My Accents™ Silver
My Accents™ White
Embossing Set

WINNING LAYOUT (page 114)

Tip & Technique - Dry Embossing

Beautiful raised patterns are easily created with the dry-embossing technique.

Step 1: With a craft mat protecting your table, place your desired stencil on top of your paper. (Brass stencils work especially well for dry-embossing.)

Step 2: Using a dry-embossing stylus, hold the stencil and paper steady and trace the stencil onto your paper.

Step 3: Remove your stencil, turn your paper over and see the finished, raised design.

Recipe

Seafoam Fleurs des Jardins™ Papers
Lilac Mist Fleurs des Jardins™ Papers
Colonial White Cardstock
Amethyst Cardstock
Vellum
Poetry in Motion Brass Stencil
My Accents™ Pewter
Spring Iris Grosgrain Ribbon
Ivory Organdy Ribbon
Fancy Cuts Bookplates

DYNAMIC DESIGN (page 116)

Tip & Technique - Coluzzle® Templates

Cutting out shapes and letters is faster, simpler, and easier using Coluzzle templates. You can quickly cut several shapes for a repeating pattern or create a page title in no time!

Step 1: Lay your paper on top of an Easy Glide™ Cutting Mat. Lay your Coluzzle template on top of the paper.

Step 2: Insert the blade of a Coluzzle® Swivel Knife into the appropriate template "track" and, holding the paper and template firmly, cut the desired shape, keeping your swivel knife in a straight-up position with your wrist and hand steady as you cut (the blade swivels to match the direction of the cut).

Step 3: Using scissors, gently snip away the remaining space of the shape.

Recipe

Heaven Sent My Stickease™ Assortment
Heavenly Blue Cardstock
Breeze Cardstock
Star Spangled Blue Cardstock
Dutch Blue Cardstock
Vellum
Block Shadow Alphabet Stencil
Paper Square Tags
White Daisy Organdy Ribbon
My Accents™ Buttercup
My Accents™ Colonial White
Coluzzle® Circle
Coluzzle® Cutting Mat
Coluzzle® Swivel Knife

GIVE ME TEN (page 118)

Tip & Technique - Anchor Journaling with Accents

Your journaling will never get lost if it is anchored with a cute coordinating embellishment!

Recipe

Summer Harvest Paper Packet
Colonial White Cardstock
Olive Exclusive Inks™ Pad
My Accents™ Garden Green
Stipple Brush

The artwork featured in *Cherish* was made using products available from Close To My Heart. The following Close To My Heart trademarks are owned by CTMH Co.: Close To My Heart®, CTMH®, Exclusive Inks™, Fleurs des Jardins™, My Accents™, My Acrylix™, My Legacy™, My Legacy Writer®, My Reflections™, My Reflections Collection™, My Stickease™, Reflections Scrapbook Program™, Sassy Strands™ and Sculpting Foam™, among others. Coluzzle®, Easy Glide™ and Guarded™ products are sourced from Provo Craft. Empressor® products are sourced from Chatterbox, LLC/EK Success, Ltd. Liquid Appliqué™ is a product of Uchida®.

© 2005 JRL PUBLICATIONS